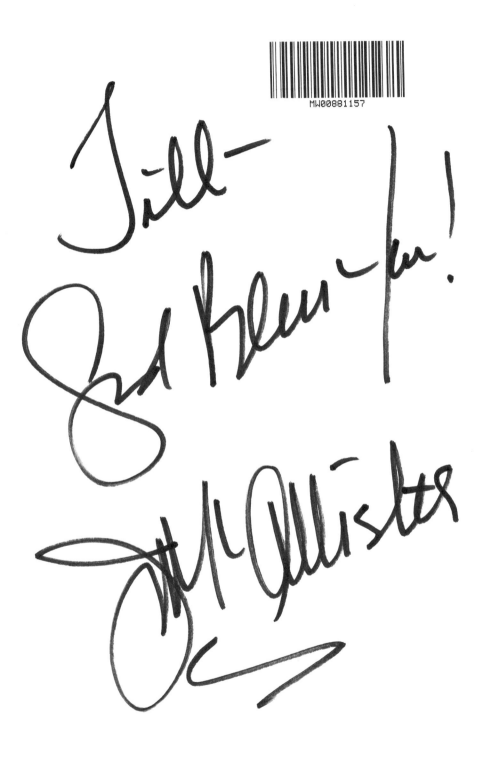

M.O.M & P.O.P

Minister of Music
&
Pastor of the People

*A Vital Relationship
for
Successful Music Ministry*

By
JUDITH
McALLISTER

Judith McAllister
PUBLISHING

M.O.M & P.O.P

Minister of Music
&
Pastor of the People

A Vital Relationship
for
Successful Music Ministry

Published by Judith McAllister Publishing
4858 West Pico Blvd Suite 755
Los Angeles, CA. 90019

Unless otherwise noted, all scriptures quotations are from the Holy Bible:
King James Version, public domain
New King James Version. Copyright © 1982 by Thomas Nelson, Inc.
Used by permission. All rights reserved.
New Century Version. Copyright © 2005 by Thomas Nelson, Inc.
Used by permission. All rights reserved.

Credits:
Editor: Judith McAllister
Editing Assistants: Antracia Morrings, Audrea Walker, Denise Gibbs
Cover Design: Emmanuel Aryee

International Standard Book Number
979-8-8623101-9-1

Visit the Author's Website

www.neverendingworship.org

TABLE OF CONTENTS

    Bishop Charles E. Blake, Sr.
    Presiding Bishop Emeritus, Church of God in Christ, Inc.
    Pastor Emeritus, West Angeles Church of God in Christ

DEDICATION

Posthumously, to the pastor whom I had the honor of "sitting under" as a child, Dr. Edward H. Boyce, founder of the Manhattan Bible Institute and Holy Tabernacle (Harlem, NY), who instilled in me a love for studying the Word of God.

To my father, the late Bishop Richard F. Christie Sr., my very first Bible teacher, who taught me how to "note the text" for intricacies within the scriptures. To my dear Mother, the late Dr. Clarice I. Christie, who taught me that "nothing is impossible with God!"

This book is also dedicated to the men and women of God; the Generals from whom I had the honor to observe, serve and glean from:

The late Oral Roberts - of whom I had the awesome, once in a lifetime privilege of observing up close, during my years of study at Oral Roberts University. While working as a television singer on the daily "LIVE" television program, I had the opportunity to spend time with him and so many other great and notable men and women of God of that time. That season in my life is indelibly etched in time as the inception of my full recognition of my destiny.

Thank you, President Roberts, for your impartation!

To the late Bishop Ernestine Reems-Dickerson - who taught us to continue on until; Bishop Jackie McCullough; what an exceptional navigator through the Word of God; Dr. Mark Hanby, Pastor Wanda Davis Turner, Bishop Joseph Warren Walker III, the late Bishop Benjamin F. Reid,

Bishop Kenneth Ulmer, Bishop Cynthia James, Bishop David and Pastor Claudette Copeland, Pastor Floyd and Co-Pastor Elaine Flake, the late Pastor Billy Joe Daughtery (Tulsa, OK), Pastor & Lady Hill – Northside Christian Center COGIC (Tulsa, Ok), Bishop Jerry Maynard - Cathedral of Praise COGIC (Nashville, TN), Bishop Felton Smith - New Covenant Holy Temple COGIC. (Nashville, TN)

General Board Members, the late Bishop George Dallas McKinney, (San Diego, CA) and the late Bishop Frank Otha White (Freeport, NY); the original leaders of the Worship Planning Commission for the annual Holy Convocation of the COGIC.

Last but certainly not by any means least, to my Spiritual Father, Bishop Charles E. Blake, Sr. – Presiding Bishop Emeritus of the Churches of God in Christ International and Pastor Emeritus of the West Angeles COGIC. (Los Angeles, CA). The impact you and Lady Mae have had on my life and ministry is immeasurable. I am so grateful!

THANK YOU!

Acknowledgments

Thank you to the following individuals who have
continually and faithfully lifted the load.

My Husband –
Darin McAllister – Thank you for being my rock and consistency!
I love and adore you!

My Arrows -
Michael, Christina, Destiny – I am so proud of each of you!
The world awaits your emergence! I believe God!

The Inner Sanctum Prayer Circle -
No need to list names - You know who you are - Thank you for
praying me through all these years!

The Intercessor Arise Family –
Seventeen years of prayer and consecration will yield great fruit
for the Kingdom! Our time is NOW!

Audrea Walker –
Your encouragement means the WORLD to me! Thank you for
your initial edits and putting up with my dangling participles

Antracia Moorings & Denise Gibbs
Thank you for coming through at the 11th hour (smile)

Vandalyn Kennedy –
Thank you for reminding me of the "Why"

Audra Christie –
My Sister in Love – I got it done Sis!

To each Pastor & Minister of Music whom I have had the
opportunity to encounter, thank you for the interaction.

I am better because of you!

FOREWORD

by Bishop Charles E. Blake, Sr.
Presiding Bishop Emeritus, Church of God in Christ, Inc.
Senior Pastor, Emeritus West Angeles Church.

When I became Pastor of West Angeles Church, we immediately began a quest for the lyrical content and sound which would characterize the life and worship of our congregation.

We sought songs that met the criteria of Ephesians 4:18-21, " but be filled with the Spirit, speaking to one another in psalms and hymns and spiritual songs, singing and making melody in your heart to the Lord, giving thanks always for all things to God the Father in the name of our Lord Jesus Christ, submitting to one another in the fear of God."

We were driven to find and occasionally compose songs and orchestrate music by which West Angeles Church was to be identified.

As we made this our mission, our congregation grew, and it became very evident to me that we were on the cusp of something great. I continued to share and preach on the ideologies of this new paradigm of worship and endeavored to set a benchmark from which others would glean and be blessed.

The following foundational principles regarding our music within the sacred space of worship in the church, are ones which were repeatedly shared with our Music Department in the early days of navigating through what I sensed God shifting West Angeles into; and these principles still work today –

OUR SONG

1. Our song should directly relate with our purpose.
2. The song should emerge from a biblical truth.
3. The song should be worthwhile.
4. Our songs should meet a need.
5. It must have literary style and worth.
6. It should show the dignity and greatness of our God.
7. It must be simple and easy enough for the congregation to pick up.
8. It must not have lyrics that are overly repetitive.
9. It should be short (some songs), but a praise song should be longer.
10. It should have a melody that is appropriate for the words.
11. It must have class and dignity.
12. It ought not be dependent on noise and accompaniment.
13. It should be appropriate for the group singing.
14. It must be within the realm of the musical ability of those singing it.

It was of paramount importance to me that we, the people of the diaspora, did not abandon what had historically brought us musically to that time, place, and season, but that we would also embrace the "new thing" that God was strategically moving us into.

While we were moving very successfully in that direction, God began to add to our arsenal, individuals who would assist us in moving our endeavor forward with precision, excellence, and anointing.

I first became aware of Judy during my visits to Oral Roberts University as a member of the Board of Directors. It was there that she, as a student, also ministered as a singer on the daily "Live" television program.

She later visited Los Angeles with plans to marry a young minister who was beginning his career as a clergyman. Once here, married and settled, Judy joined the staff of West Angeles working in our Membership Services Department and participated in the existing Music Department. She served faithfully and humbly.

However, as I observed her and her participation in our music ministry, it was clear to me that God was calling her to serve as a leader of worship in the life of West Angeles.

We spoke frequently, sharing the vision for the music that would offer a sacrifice of worship and praise to God, and inspire, edify, and empower our congregation.

We have actively sought to maintain unwavering biblical and spiritual content. Judith McAllister and our previous Ministers of Music have all joined in this endeavor.

A primary result is a higher level of worship and praise because the people of the Lord were called upon to sing unto the Lord new songs with new understanding and new power.

Her service to God and the effectiveness of her worship leadership at West Angeles was such that it was my joy to appoint her as The President and Minister of Music for the International Music Department for the duration of my tenure as Presiding Bishop of the Church of God in Christ, Inc.

Her impact on the ministry of Praise & Worship and Gospel Music is undeniable, and she is a great blessing to us all.

THANK YOU JUDITH MCALLISTER
FOR A GREAT BOOK!

Introduction

The woman of God I am today can be attributed to the many experiences that I've encountered over my lifetime - some good, others unpleasant, but all working together for my ultimate good (Romans 8:28).

As I recall the events that have played a tremendous part in fashioning me, my ministry mindset and disposition, I must note that I have been blessed above measure to have worked with and under the visionary leadership of Bishop Charles E. Blake Sr., Presiding Bishop Emeritus for the Churches of God in Christ International, and Pastor Emeritus of the West Angeles Church of God in Christ (Los Angeles, CA).

While serving cumulatively as Worship Leader for twenty-three years and Executive Director (or for the purpose of this book, Minister of Music) of the Music & Worship Arts Ministry for twenty years, I had the opportunity to become acquainted with leadership excellence at its finest. Many of the principles shared in this book are direct reflections of philosophies gleaned while serving at West Angeles Church.

I arrived at West Angeles in August of 1988, fresh out of college and newly married. Never in my wildest dreams would I have ever imagined that my arrival at West Angeles would set my life on trajectory for life transformation.

Allow me to give perspective …. I grew up in a very strict Pentecostal Holiness background where much of our extra-curricular activities consisted of playing double-dutch and hopscotch in the street in front of our house - in a skirt mind you and making sure we were in the house before the streetlights came on.

It is against this backdrop that I graduated from the High School for the Performing Arts (Manhattan, NY) at the age of sixteen. My father wished for me to remain in New York to assist him in ministry, so I attended State University of New York At Old Westbury, a college not too far from home, so I could come home on the weekends.

But after three years, of the back and forth and finding no satisfaction or significant spiritual growth, I was encouraged by my mother to change my environment. The deep dive of research began, and I decided to transfer to Oral Roberts University (ORU) in Tulsa Oklahoma.

In obedience to God, I left all I knew behind and went to follow the inner "knowing", that God had something better for me, and that somehow, I would end up in Los Angeles, California.

It was at Oral Roberts University that I answered my call to the ministry of Praise & Worship. Subsequent to that "yes", I had the opportunity to become acquainted with the late Dr. Myles Monroe, who totally revolutionized my life and ministry by sharing amongst other truths, the revelation of the "The Seven Levels of Praise".

In addition, the opportunity to be one of the singers on *Richard Roberts Live* daily television program provided the honor of interfacing with a great number of the Generals of the faith of that day.

My fiancée, Darin McAllister, was responsible for working the audience during the show as well as securing transportation for its high-profile guests. It was here that he met Bishop Charles E. Blake, Sr., upon one of his visits to the University. Bishop Blake asked Darin if he had any plans after graduation and invited him to come and visit West Angeles to see if that might be a consideration. Well – the rest as they say is history.

I married Darin in 1988 and off we went to Los Angeles California, where Darin served Bishop Blake as his personal aide at the West Angeles Church of God in Christ.

When I arrived at West Angeles, I took my time joining the music ministry. Instead, I became involved right away in the day-to-day life of the church by volunteering my time in the Membership and Support Services Department and was eventually hired on as the Church Receptionist.

There were at least six choirs in West Angeles at the time, and I wanted to ensure before joining any one of them, that I had joined the right one because once I make a commitment, I desired to honor it!

Sitting in the audience was a bit strange for me because even as a child, I was always on the platform involved in some facet of ministry. So, I sat in the audience Sunday after Sunday, in the 1,200 seat auditorium, observing the various musical approaches of the various musical aggregations that would suit the multi-service crowds.

My arrival to West Angeles was right on the cusp of the church expanding to the point that an additional service had to be added to the existing two. The new schedule was 7:00am, 9:00am and 11:00am, in addition to a 7:00pm Service.

The services were executed with precision where there was no "fat" because there was not time for that. People were lined up outside of the building all the way down the street waiting to enter to worship by the time the first service had concluded.

The music was excellent, and the Word of God was exceptional. It was an example of the marriage of Music Ministry & the Word at its finest.

Patrick Henderson, who at that time was the Minister of Music, knew that I was familiar with the type of music and the direction in which Bishop Blake was desirous of taking the congregation - because of my affiliation with ORU and the music ministered daily on the television program.

One Sunday, after participating in the choir for about four months, Patrick asked me to lead the congregation in a worship song "Here we are in Your Presence, lifting holy hands to You". To this day, I can recall the looks on the faces of many in the congregation when he and I began to sing. Many had scowls on their faces because they didn't quite understand what was taking place. The music was unfamiliar, new, and unlike what they were accustomed to. Patrick and I pressed through and made it through the song.

After that particular service, one of the high-ranking staff members of the church approached me, put their hand on my shoulder and said, "Don't ask us to stand, or to lift our hands, we are not white." Truthfully, that comment caused me quite a bit of angst, because I did not view that song as a white or black song, but a song of praise unto God from a grateful heart.

Those days of transition and introducing something new were filled with a great deal of pushback, and a great deal of misunderstanding regarding the purpose of what it was we were endeavoring to accomplish.

Members of the choir were upset because this new form of music was taking up some of the time that would have ordinarily been given to them to minister in song. Remember, we only had so much time given the fact that there were multiple services taking place in one day. Some church members were afraid that we would abandon the traditional good ole foot stomping, handclapping, and jubilant presentations, for songs they did not care for or that would not make them "shout". And boy – did they write letters about their displeasure!

It seemed as if Patrick and I, and a few other key individuals were marching up a hill with no end in sight.

But we persevered!

After three years of what felt like plowing, by conducting workshops, teaching and training choir members, and forming a worship team (from those in the congregation who, without coercion, stood in the presence of the Lord during the Praise & Worship segment of our services), Patrick and his team at Sparrow Records, produced a groundbreaking project entitled "Saints In Praise", which spoke to the vision in Bishop Blake's heart, as he "continued to preach on the ideologies of this new paradigm and shift in worship, and set a benchmark by which others would glean from and be blessed by". (*Bishop Charles E. Blake, Sr. – Foreword*)

Patrick and the musicians recorded the music in the studio, brought the instrumental tracks to the church, and during our Pastors' Bible Study one Thursday evening, recorded both the choir and the congregation singing songs of praise unto the Lord.

"Saints In Praise" spread like wildfire! It gave the people whose faces had been kissed by the sun, an additional form of musical expression in worship. This musical expression of "praise and worship" was nothing new in the Black Church – we have done it for centuries. Many called it "devotional service" in their times gathering to worship. The practice of call and response, or antiphonal singing, originated in Africa. We have **always** understood that we must sing!

What the "Saints in Praise" series did, was give the song back to the people in the congregation – at a time when choirs and specialized groups were abounding.

Intricate harmonies, vocal placements, and beats were the primary calling card of many of these musical aggregations and music ministries all over the country endeavoring to sound just like their favorite choir or group heard on the radio.

As the years passed, what resulted was that the congregation, who once actively participated the service, now began to just sit, and watch these wonderful choirs and excellent groups sing as opposed to participating in the worship.

Let me pause here and state that there is absolutely nothing wrong with excellent groups and choirs; excellence in music ministry must be our aim – ALWAYS. However, in the worship setting, our aim as the music ministry is to create an atmosphere conducive for two things to transpire:

(1) The people taking ownership of their worship.
(2) The presence of God dwelling and moving among His people.

A few months after the release of "Saints in Praise – Volume 1", we received numerous reports from churches that did not have musicians or singers, that they would actually play the album over their speaker system, and the congregation would stand and sing along. They would sing to the whole first side of the album!

At that time, a majority of our black congregations did not stand, move, or dance unless they were prompted to do so by the "quickening" of the Spirit, but Bishop Blake had a vision of the congregation engaging at will in worship unto God. We would often say to our music staff:

"The song of worship must be given back to the people; they are to sing unto the Lord. The choir must not hold the song hostage, the people must not be so enamored by the choir that they do not sing. I see **OUR** *people, standing, with their hands lifted in praise unto the Lord".*

The ministry impact that I have been blessed to accomplish in Praise & Worship is due in large part, to the teachings, impartation, encouragement and loving correction of my Pastor, Bishop Charles E. Blake, Sr. The Kingdom partnership we were able to forge for over thirty-five years has changed the face of the ministry of worship as we know it, and it is primarily from the vantage point of this relationship that this book is penned.

The relationship between Pastor and Minister of Music is one where there must be a unification of thought, vision, mutual respect, and an alignment of purpose.

When the words 'Mom' and 'Pop' are mentioned, it invokes a mental picture of a mother and father, heading a household of children. Similarly, the interconnection between the Minister of Music (M.O.M.) and the Pastor of the People (P.O.P.) is important for the balance of music ministry and the Word of God.

The Music Ministry should be crafted so the environment is conducive to planting the seed of the Word of God into the hearts of the people, which is the most important part of any worship service.

What I have learned over my forty-plus years in this facet of ministry, I now share with you, and I pray that the lessons and principles in this book will serve as encouragement to you – helping you understand to some degree both the roles of M.O.M. and P.O.P., and why Ministers of Music are vital to the success of facilitating the atmosphere for worship.

At the end of each chapter, you are encouraged to take a few moments to "Selah". Before going to the next chapter, pause, think, and reflect on what you have read by asking yourself some poignant questions….

- How does this chapter speak to me?

- How can I apply what I have learned to my current situation?

- What is God calling me to do as a result of having received this information?

Allow those questions to raise your awareness and clarity about who you are, Whose you are and who you have been called to serve.

I believe in you!

Let us pray.

Father, I bring to You my fellow laborer in the Kingdom, whom You have directed to pick up this book.

I pray that You will allow them to be quickened and illuminated by Your Word, which will yield wisdom and insight into the areas of ministry unto which You have called them.

Holy Spirit, speak to them beyond the words of these pages; as they are reading, allow them to have visions and insights concerning how they are to navigate in ministry during these times and seasons.

Father, so much is changing, shifting and unknown; but when we don't know what to do, thank You that we can indeed run to You.

I pray that You would grant unto Your servants, knowledge of witty inventions, and the ability to articulate Heaven's worship, here on earth.

Let Your will be done and let Your Kingdom come. In Jesus' mighty and strong name …..

Amen.

A WORD

TO THE
PASTOR

A WORD
TO THE PASTOR

A balanced family is one of the by-products of a healthy relationship between a husband and a wife.

As it is in the natural, so it is in the spiritual. For the sake of this literary offering, the typology of a successful music ministry requires, among other key and important elements, a healthy relationship between the M.O.M. (*Minister of Music*) and P.O.P. (*Pastor of the People*).

From the perspective of one who has served in the role of Minister of Music for many years, allow me to offer a few initial suggestions, which hopefully will contribute to the strength and success of this vital Kingdom relationship.

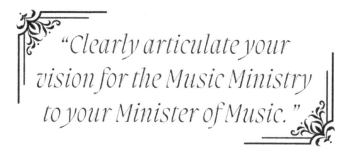

"Clearly articulate your vision for the Music Ministry to your Minister of Music."

Firstly, I encourage you to clearly articulate your vision for the Music Ministry to your Minister of Music. He or she needs to understand your vision for the sound of the house and the role that they will play in working towards its fulfillment.

Secondly, be aware of the misconception that worship leadership is the sole responsibility of your Minister of Music. As the 'Angel of the House', **you** serve as the primary Worship Leader of your congregation.

You may not sing or play an instrument; but everything that transpires in the house flows from you – just as the activity in a healthy home flows from the God-ordained head of the family.

In my many years of travel and consulting with various ministries across a broad spectrum of religious organizations and denominations, I have observed that often, pastors do not fully comprehend their role as the primary worship leader. They proceed to delegate "that" responsibility to others, and then wonder why their congregation does not readily enter into the presence of God when He responds to our praise. These pastors remain in their offices during the worship/music portions of their services and don't understand that it is vital for the congregation to see its leader present, worshiping and participating. As the Pastor goes, so goes the church!

It is important that you exemplify and impart into your music ministry what you desire to see, by the demonstration of your worship.

Thirdly, it is beneficial to periodically interface with your Minister of Music. Endeavor to spend time with those who give "food" to your congregation. The Word of God is obviously and must always remain the priority in a service; but the music ministry ranks very closely in importance.

Music is so important to God that it is mentioned in one form or another, over five hundred times in the scriptures. God places emphasis on that which is most important to Him. We are even commanded to *"come before His presence with singing."* (Psalm 100:2 KJV)

While preaching, praying, and prophesying will cease in heaven (I Corinthians 13:8), worship will continue on for eternity (Revelation 4:8-11); so, our understanding of worship must be developed while here on the earth. Our desire ought to be to become effective in our worship, and model that aspect of worship before those whom we have been charged to shepherd.

In the relationship between M.O.M. and P.O.P. one of the means for effectiveness is communication. It is in this light that I suggest regular meetings with your M.O.M. which will facilitate your united effort to bring the congregation to a level of worship that is pleasing unto God and beneficial to them. So much deliverance and breakthrough can be achieved in the presence of the Lord!

It is my prayer that in reading this book, you will gain greater clarity on the function of a Minister of Music, and that you will the allow them the latitude to fulfill their role in assisting you in facilitating, and interpreting to the congregation, the vision that God has sovereignly placed in your spirit.

Be encouraged – because help is on the way!

A WORD

TO THE MINISTER OF MUSIC

A WORD
TO THE MINISTER OF MUSIC

As Ministers of Music (M.O.M), we know how to teach a song, we can direct a choir, we can play the latest chords and instruct our singers and musicians. Many of us hold degrees in music from the finest schools and institutions of higher learning, some of us are gifted songwriters; but none of these things, in and of themselves, can revolutionize the worship that takes place in our churches.

In addition to all of the obvious elements that must be honed to foster success, a healthy relationship with your Pastor is a key component to the effectiveness of your music ministry and overall success of your service within the church.

In the natural, a marriage begins with the likelihood of a man and a woman making the decision to join in holy matrimony. Following the splendor of the honeymoon, the period of newness wears off and real life kicks in. This is when the couple discovers that a marriage is not only the union of two people, but also the collision of two worlds with two ideologies and various frames of reference.

The merge is not always smooth, but to maintain harmony and unity, the one whom God has ordained as the head of the household must lead well; and the one whom God has called to help must yield and submit to the vision.

Failure, on the part of either party, to fulfill his/her role will result in dysfunction which opens the door for problems down the line.

The same applies to the M.O.M. and P.O.P. relationship. Adherence to the Biblical principle of submission to leadership; while unpopular in this culture and certainly unsettling to the ego, will not only provide the joy of unity and fellowship but it will create an environment where God will move mightily.

My goal in writing this book is to provide enlightenment regarding the role of the Minister of Music and, in doing so, address the root of many problems which exist within our Music & Creative Arts ministries today.

Be encouraged – because help is on the way!

CHAPTER ONE

PRINCIPLES FOR SUCCESS

THE DOOR

In the book of Revelation 3:20, Jesus said,

> *"Behold, I stand at the **door**, and knock: if any man hear my voice, and open the **door**, I will come in to him, and will sup with him, and he with me."*

Here we observe the picture of Jesus standing on the outside of the structure waiting for those on the inside to hear His voice and make the decision to open the door and let Him in. In this instance, the door symbolizes an opportunity for change, transition, and a choice to begin again. They had a choice, whether or not to allow Him into their space to bring things into order.

In Nehemiah's account of rebuilding the wall of Jerusalem, he states:

> *"...I had rebuilt the wall ... but I had not yet set the doors in the gates"* (**Nehemiah 6:1, New Century Version**).

Consider the detriment of building a structure to house and protect a family, a structure to secure precious items, but a structure devoid of that which would keep all of it safe - - the door! There must be some sort of mechanism to keep what is inside the structure secure as well as prevent the entry of that which is undesired.

"This is the season for the doors to be re-hung."

Many of our great predecessors who functioned in the ministry of music, those who have paved the way as it relates to the comprehension of the importance and significance of music ministry have, in a sense, built the wall.

Conversely, if we take a serious look at what has been coined as music ministry particularly in today's Western World, we will unfortunately observe such an egregious display of performance-driven competition, service which is not motivated by humility, faithfulness, or the comprehension of assignment, but rather, motivated by a desire for the spotlight, self-centeredness, and an ambition to "get the house" as opposed to getting the heart of God.

These, as well as other negative concepts from the world's system, have warped the understanding of what God truly desires; and this in turn, has led to performance-driven mindsets, polluted worship, and a breach in the Spirit causing a feel-good environment with no power of God demonstrated - because someone has failed to 'hang the doors.

This is the season for the doors to be re-hung. It's time to re-establish boundaries and re-discover what God's Word admonishes us to allow in or keep out. We must recall and practice the precepts and perspectives necessary to assist us in maintaining a healthy view of what music ministry truly is.

It is within this framework that we must open our hearts to receive the instructions necessary to direct us in what to allow in, what to release, which ideals to embrace and which concepts and attitudes to reject.

The door is necessary and those who have been given the responsibility to steward it, are held to a high standard to ensure that what enters as well as exits, ebbs and flows from it, is conducive and necessary for both the growth and safety of those who are on the inside of the structure.

With this in mind, we will examine a few principles which establish parameters for a productive relationship between the Pastor and Minister of Music and their collaborative effort to man "The Door".

THE HANDLE

Picture in your mind a briefcase, suitcase, and a purse. Each is them intentionally designed to carry important items on the inside. The contents of the briefcase, suitcase and purse may be very different; but no matter how expensive or inexpensive the bag is, what is on the inside of that bag is more important than the bag itself.

Designer bags, although very expensive and symbolic of luxury and affluence, are simply receptacles crafted to aid an individual in carrying numerous articles and attached to each briefcase, suitcase and purse is usually a handle that allows the bag to be carried with ease.

"Music Ministry" is much like "The Handle". The handle alone, existing apart from the item it was designed to be attached to, does no one any good. The handle is provided to evenly distribute the weight of the contents of the bag.

For our purposes in this analogy, the Word of God is likened unto the bag, and the contents of the bag are representative of the blessings, miracles, signs, and wonders that are in the Word of God for his people to access.

So, we see that Music Ministry, just for music ministry's sake, is not what the Kingdom is calling for. Our music MUST be attached to the Word of God and must take second place to the Word of God.

We must minister and sing songs that reflect of the Word, the will, and the counsel of God. In addition, 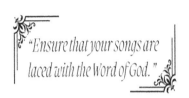 allow me to admonish the M.O.M.s who are songwriters – make sure that your songs are laced with the Word of God.

It is the Word that has the staying power, the ability to transform lives and deliver the hearts of men; and when you infuse the Word of God with music, you have a very powerful tool to bring healing, deliverance, lifting and all the things that the Father wants to download to His children.

It is the Word that will never pass away, and Jesus said in Matthew 24:35 - **Heaven and earth** *shall pass away, but my words shall not pass away.*

If at all possible, meet with your Pastor to ascertain the general thought and mindset of what will be preached, so that you, M.O.M., will be able to prepare the music to serve as 'the handle'. The congregation may not always remember the preached word-for-word; but they will remember a song that is connected to the Word, thus bringing them back TO the spoken Word.

Thus, a level of healthy eating is maintained by not only being fed verbally (through the P.O.P.'s message), but also musically (via the M.O.M.'s ministry).

If the P.O.P. is providing a rich banquet of food, but the M.O.M. is derelict in his/her duties by inappropriately crafting the handle, it will create more work and stress on both P.O.P. and the congregation.

In the natural, children who aren't sustained by a proper diet face all kinds of deficiencies and ailments. M.O.M. and P.O.P. must implement and work together to present the same spiritual nutritional plan. Whatever provision "Dad" gives is the basis for "Mom's" meals, and this facilitates the growth of a healthy environment in addition to healthy children.

"In likening this spiritual relationship to the natural relationship, we will see how the joining together in spirit can yield a healthy and productive army of children."

A healthy church is one that is always growing – not just in numbers, but in maturation among its members. With the passing of each year, the parishioners of a healthy church will show marked improvement in their level of maturity; and the amount of "foolishness" seen in past years will diminish.

When the M.O.M. understands that his/her role is as important (*in terms of dedication, consecration, study, knowledge of Word, and most importantly being able to articulate all of that in the music*) - as the P.O.P.'s role, a healthy interaction will transpire.

AGREEMENT

The Encarta World English Dictionary defines agreement as:

1. A contract or arrangement, either written or verbal and sometimes enforceable by law.
2. The reaching or sharing of the same opinion that somebody or others hold.
3. A situation in which everyone accepts the same terms or has the same opinion.

The function of Minister of Music is one that must be approached with recognition of a key principle.

> *Walking in agreement and alignment with the Pastor's vision for the music ministry is not only vital for the success of the ministry, but a responsibility, as the M.O.M. is a notable support for the ministry at large.*

Pursuant to this acknowledgment, the M.O.M. should possess qualities, that will put the P.O.P at ease – knowing that the M.O.M. is committed to the task at hand, not only because of the assignment, but also because there is a genuine love for God and dedication to the leader, the congregation, and the ministry.

Two cannot walk together unless they agree (Amos 3:3) and are able to work together effectively; and while the M.O.M. may be talented and able to do the job, problems are inevitable if the P.O.P's heart and vision are not at the forefront of the M.O.M's mind.

In biblical times, there were two primary ways utilized to grind wheat which was needed for making bread.

1) Women used a pestle and mortar, for smaller jobs.

2) Oxen, tethered at the neck by a yoke on the threshing floor, pulled a large wide wheel to separate large quantities of the wheat from the chaff.

These oxen would walk together in a circle , and the same rate and speed, to remove the chaff from the wheat and crush the grain into the essential elements necessary to make flour for bread.

The oxen were the same height, which was necessary to alleviate strain on either of their necks. In essence, they stood shoulder to shoulder. Yoking oxen of different sizes would present a problem, as the yoke on the neck of the smaller ox would pull on the neck of the larger ox because of gravity.

This would also present a problem for the smaller ox in that it would have to assume weight on its neck that it was not mature or strong enough to carry.

I have seen this proverbial picture play out many more times than I would care to mention. For M.O.M. and P.O.P. to be equally yoked, M.O.M. must be strong enough to handle his/her portion of the spiritual warfare that is inevitable when pursing Kingdom vision.

This is one of the reasons why it is important for the M.O.M. to have not only a proficiency in the art of music, but also a life of consecration and dedication to the Word of God.

The M.O.M. is usually tasked with the role of leading and cultivating a group of "warriors" in Music Ministry - a company of Levities, who have been assigned to prepare an atmosphere conducive for the presence of God to dwell.

In addition to this, it is of great importance that there is agreement, synergy, and an understanding of the assignment between the M.O.M. and P.O.P. because when spiritual warfare commences it's too late to try to figure out what to do.

The fight will be on!

You see, the opposing forces of the Kingdom of God will always attempt to create hindrances to ministerial success, and because we are not ignorant of the enemy's devices (2 Corinthians 2:11b) M.O.M. and P.O.P. must posture themselves to mitigate the desire of his plan!

Coming into agreement with consistent communication, clear articulation and rehearsing of the vision will aid in eradicating confusion and the sense of uncertainty that may arise when one does not understand what is expected.

SUBMISSION

Once the P.O.P. has clearly articulated the vision, it is incumbent upon the M.O.M. that they submit to that vision and do everything within his/her given line of authority to ensure that this vision is manifested.

Many have come to believe that the word submission must be interpreted as one individual becoming subservient to another. This belief system is incorrect and distant from what God intends submission to look like.

Love is the initial factor in producing the response of submission. When there is love and respect for the one to whom we submit, it is "love" which will prompt an appropriate response. Ministry will be a bit easier to facilitate, if there is an agape love which flows from P.O.P. to flock and vice versa. As P.O.P. loves the flock, the people will, in turn, respond with love and submit to P.O.P. and the vision.

In addition to submitting as a response to love; we also submit in order to grow. The Word declares that God has given apostles, prophets, evangelists, pastors, and teachers for "*the perfecting of the saints… till we all come in the unity of the faith*" (Ephesians 4:11-13, KJV).

Some believe that apostles do not exist today; but I would ask: Have we come into that "*perfecting*" yet? Have we all "*come into the unity of faith*"? God has placed these authorities and gifts in His church, to whom we must submit for our growth and development.

There are instances where the Father allows us to be confronted with situations and environments where we can choose to make the experience an opportunity for growth or choose to walk in unforgiveness and be overtaken with bitterness.

There will be times when M.O.M. will not always agree with P.O.P., and in those times, the purpose and the vision need to be indelibly etched in their spirits, so when those rough times arise, there is still clarity and no movement away from what God said.

Psalm 37:23 reminds us that *"the steps of a good man are ordered by the Lord….."* Often, a person will not appreciate his current circumstances and decide to vacate the

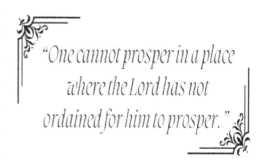

"One cannot prosper in a place where the Lord has not ordained for him to prosper."

place that has been ordered by God; but it is important to note that a person cannot grow in a place where the Lord has not planted them. One cannot prosper in a place where the Lord has not ordained for him to prosper.

A MOM cannot flourish at a church, or in a space where God has not called them to be. Thus, it is imperative to remain in the place of assignment until the Lord indicates that you have completed the assignment. This will often be evident in that the Lord will provide a clear path for transition to the next assignment.

Submission is also a critical component in the fight against what I term as the "Lucifer mentality:"

> *"How you are fallen from heaven, O Lucifer… For you have said in your heart: '**I will** ascend into heaven, **I will** exalt my throne above the stars of God; **I will** also sit on the mount of the congregation … **I will** ascend above the heights of the clouds, **I will** be like the Most High."(Isaiah 14:12-14, NKJV – emphasis added)*

The premise of this mentality is pride, and "*Pride goes before destruction, and a haughty spirit before a fall*". (Proverbs 16:18) This mentality wants all the attention and all the shine. It says – "I'm just as good as, if not better than the one whom I have been called to assist…" It manifests in the M.O.M. who says "Look at what I can do…. I have these people in the palm of my hands…. I can *"shift the house"* better and with more charisma than P.O.P. can."

Although this may be a factual element due to the emotive nature of music and the effect that it has on individuals, the truth is that this posture reflects a spirit of pride to which one has fallen prey! Lucifer was lifted up in pride due to his exquisite appearance and musical giftings:

"Thou hast been in Eden the garden of God; every precious stone was thy covering, the sardius, topaz, and the diamond, the beryl, the onyx, and the jasper, the sapphire, the emerald, and the carbuncle, and gold: the workmanship of thy tabrets and of thy pipes was prepared in thee in the day that thou wast created. Thou art the anointed cherub that covereth; and I have set thee so: thou wast upon the holy mountain of God; thou hast walked up and down in the midst of the stones of fire."
(Ezekiel 28:13-14, KJV)

Just as light shining through a prism brings forth a bouquet of beautiful colors, I would imagine that the light of God (Revelation 21:23, 22:5) shone through Lucifer's precious stones making him even more beautiful.

Could it be that Lucifer became distracted by his own attractiveness and ability, and he forgot the source of his beauty and skill? Could it be that many of today's music ministers are filled with pride, because of the fact that their gifts can shift and change atmospheres?

The M.O.M. must bear in mind that they are there to support and submit to the leadership and vision of P.O.P., and their gifts are to be used for the support of both. The M.O.M. should be focused on the vision of the Pastor with no hidden agendas.

By 'hidden agendas,' I'm referring to building and developing their own little kingdom, while camouflaging their activity under the auspices of working for the church.

There must be the willing act of submission - submitting one's gift to the house, submitting to the will of God and submitting one's thoughts to the Word and purposes of God. This is the only way to circumvent the Lucifer mentality:

> *"For the weapons of our warfare are not carnal, but mighty through God to the pulling down of strong holds; casting down imaginations, and every high thing that exalteth itself against the knowledge of God, and bringing into captivity every thought to the obedience of Christ..."(II Corinthians 10:4-5, King James Version)*

Many won't admit it, but I will. The battle against this mindset is a constant reality. If the devil tempted Jesus, how then could we ever believe that we are exempt? We must recognize the enemy's devices (II Corinthians 2:11) and resist the ever-present temptation to cater to our egos and abandon the principle of submission.

What does submission look like?

One of the embodiments of submission is the practice of laying down one's desires for the will of another.

Matthew chapter 26 chronicles the account of Jesus preparing to face the culmination of His purpose on earth. He engaged in the Last Supper with His disciples, reminded them of His impending plight and then went to the Garden of Gethsemane to pray.

During this agonizing time in His life, we observe in verse 39 that Jesus asked for the 'cup' – The difficult experience to be removed from Him. Yet, because He understood His purpose, He submitted to his Father's will, even in the face of death:

> *Verse 39 "And he went a little farther, and fell on his face, and prayed, saying, O my Father, if it be possible, let this cup pass from me: nevertheless, not as I will, but as thou wilt."*

Jesus abandoned His will, so that His Father's desire could become a reality. Likewise, we must abandon our will for the will of the Father; The M.O.M. should yield in submission to the will and vision of the P.O.P.

SPIRITUAL AUTHORITY

"Everyone must submit to governing authorities. For all authority comes from God, and those in positions of authority have been placed there by God.
So, anyone who rebels against authority is rebelling against what God has instituted, and they will be punished." (Romans 13:1-2, NCV)

Respect for spiritual authority must be applied at all levels within the church. If a Minister of Music wants loving submission from those they lead and nurture in music ministry, then they should submit to the Pastor. If he/she wants those who serve under their leadership to do what they ask them to do, then he/she must do what the Pastor asks them to do.

The scripture declares that whatever we sow is what we will reap (Galatians 6:7), and a harvest always comes in a level of abundance which is greater than what was sown. For example, sowing a single grain of corn will eventually yield a stalk containing several ears of corn, which will house hundreds of kernels.

In the same way, the M.O.M. who wants to reap the blessing of good, cooperative staff members must be sure that he/she has sown dedicated service and consistent submission to the Pastor's authority.

All ministry gifts in the house of God are subject to the administration and governing of the shepherd of the house. The ministry and gifts of the M.O.M. are to be submitted to assist the Man or Woman of God in their responsibilities and are designed to lift the burden and to make their job a little easier.

Let's examine David's relationship with King Saul. The Bible gives us several accounts where King Saul wronged David; but David did not paint a negative reflection of Saul to others and did not allow Saul's spirit to cause him to react in a wrong way. He refused to touch the Lord's anointed.

When presented with the opportunity to take Saul's life, David did not. (I Samuel 24, 26) On one occasion, he cut off a piece of Saul's garment (I Samuel 24:4). This was to show Saul that he could have killed him destroyed his reputation, and exposed to the Israelites the intimate details of what he knew about the royal family; but he did not. Why? David refrained because he respected Saul's position as the appointed and anointed leader of Israel.

A Minister of Music must submit to authority. It is a hard message, and even harder to do; but comparing today's challenges to what David went through - including the fact that Saul tried to kill him more than once - should give us hope. Even when faced with a dire situation, David stayed in submission until the Lord opened up the way for him to occupy the throne as king.

The scriptures record the tragic end to Saul's life when he went into battle and, ultimately committed suicide; but they also highlight David's respect for spiritual authority. When a young Amalekite claimed to have killed Saul, (I Samuel 31 - II Samuel 1), he met an untimely death when David issued the edict for him to be executed. *"Were you not fearful to touch the Lord's anointed?'* David asked (II Samuel 1:14).

In situations where there is turmoil in the relationship between M.O.M. and P.O.P., the M.O.M. must ensure that maturity and restraint are exemplified, rather than complaining to others and speaking against the Lord's appointed leader. He/She should instead talk the situation over with God in prayer.

While allowing God to intervene and bring resolution, it is important to follow David's example by remaining consistent in the posture of submission, honor, and respect for leadership.

SELAH

Feel free to write on this page how Chapter One spoke to you.

_____

_____

_____

_____

_____

_____

_____

_____

_____

_____

_____

_____

CHAPTER TWO

THE POWER OF VISION

In the natural, possessing 20/20 vision refers to an individual having optimal sight in both eyes, enabling them to see near and far without visual aid or assistance.

The power of clear, focused, and precise vision, understanding of one's purpose, goals, and the direction in which they are headed is a road map, that when P.O.P. delivers, all given to their care are enabled to follow.

When the MOM receives the vision from POP, it creates an atmosphere of freedom to operate within the circumference of that vision, wherein they can align their departmental goals, staff choices, and musical selections. This alignment brings a sense of fulfillment, joy, and peace and acts as a guiding compass particularly in difficult times.

When MOM and POP share a common vision speaking the same thing within a spiritual community, it creates a strong sense of unity and purpose for those who follow and model. The vision provides an understanding of the greater impact that unity can produce, which in turn will motivate and assist the congregation by igniting a desire for growth and transformation by what they see demonstrated through the power of unity.

Serving the Vision

The Word of God declares in Psalms 37:4

> *"…delight yourself also in the Lord, He will give you the desires of your heart"*

'Delight' refers to more than just praising and worshipping God, it refers to submitting wholly to Him and allowing the desire of God **FOR** us, to be revealed **IN** us. As we delight ourselves in God by working and putting our shoulders to the plow of ministry, He will not forget our labor of love (Hebrews 6:10).

More often than not, the Lord will reveal to the M.O.M "offshoots" of the Pastor's vision. *(Think of the vision as a tree, and the branches as specific ideas. The "offshoots" are the smaller branches.)* I found these "offshoots" to be aspirations in my Pastor's heart, things that he may not have had language to articulate but knew what it was when he saw it.

It behooves the M.O.M. to seek God's face to discover what He desires and after so doing, speak with the Pastor and share what God has revealed. The M.O.M. will frequently discover that the two of them are on one accord. We serve the same God; and the same God Who speaks to the Pastor, can also speak to the M.O.M.

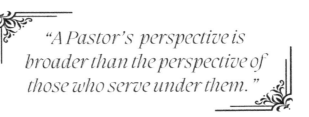

"A Pastor's perspective is broader than the perspective of those who serve under them."

It is essential, however, to remember that the Pastor knows the right timing for implementing new ideas and concepts. The Lord may have given the M.O.M. a beautiful vision; and it may be a part of the Pastor's vision for ministry that will be of benefit to the church, however, if the Pastor decides to wait, or hold off for a little while, the M.O.M. should not become discouraged.

Luke 2:19 says that *"Mary kept all these things and pondered them in her heart"* and the M.O.M. must hold on to this vision, knowing that it was given by God; but must also respect and honor the Pastor's decision regarding the timing of its implementation.

A pastor's perspective is broader than the perspective of those who serve under them. The M.O.M. deals with just one aspect of ministry, but the Pastor has to deal with all aspects. P.O.P. may see how an idea of innovation brought forth in one area might hinder an aspect of ministry in another area, so P.O.P. delays or says no, that decision ought not be taken personally.

P.O.P. knows the timing of the vision and the facts regarding the best season for its elements to come together. P.O.P. is ultimately responsible to God for the flock and must lead them in accordance with the leading of the Lord.

Although the M.O.M., in a sense, may be an 'under shepherd,' the Pastor is the God-ordained shepherd who is ultimately at the helm. It is the Pastor, not the M.O.M., who will have to answer to God when he asks: *"What have you done with my flock?"*

The Minister of Music must be submitted to the timing of the vision realizing that it is for an appointed time, and that the Pastor knows when it should be brought to fruition. In addition, we must know how to ebb, flow and shift with the Pastor, and MOM must be able to flow in sync with POP. The focus must be centered on sowing into the Pastor's vision.

Let's take a look at the life of Joseph. Joseph sowed into the visions of others. We find that Joseph sowed into the lives of Potiphar, the butler, the baker and even Pharaoh. When he served the vision of others, then the Lord allowed his dream to come to pass (Genesis 39-47). We do not see in scripture where Joseph worked on his own vision or tried to make himself great so that people would bow down to him, like he saw in this dream. He first worked on the visions of others and then his dreams were fulfilled.

The M.O.M. ought always defer to the Pastor. M.O.M. should work with diligence to make the pastoral vision come to pass, even if it means at times putting aside activities and ideas which hold personal significance. God will not forget the faithfulness and sacrifice of those who endeavor to walk in obedience to Him by serving in the house of God for the good of the Kingdom.

SHARING THE VISION

Those who serve under the Minister of Music must also have a clear understanding of the Pastor's vision, their expectations for the structure of the music ministry, music preferences, order of service, etc.; and once the M.O.M. has received that clear vision, it is their responsibility to communicate that vision clearly and concisely. The vision can be communicated through meetings, workshops or by dropping nuggets during rehearsals. It can also be as simple as the way one presents himself in being reflective of what the Pastor has spoken. Some principles are taught, and others are caught.

The team should be aware of what the Pastor desires; and the M.O.M. must direct the focus of the team and pull the skills and abilities out of each member to aid in fulfilling the Pastor's wishes.

As an example, I observed that my leader did not care too much for songs with repetitive lyrics. So, I provided our choir directors with a list of items that a song should contain, very similar to the one I was provided when I was appointed Minister of Music. *(Revisit the Foreword for the list)*

As aforementioned, In the early days of the inception of the "Saints in Praise" era, Bishop Blake said to me: "I want to see **OUR** people lifting their hands in worship." He gave no other directives or specifics as to how to make that happen. Remember, worshipping with lifted hand was not a thing back then. We didn't stand in worship unless the choir gave us a "hot" song, and even then, it took some time to get them on their feet! I had to go to God and ask: "How do I make this happen?"

In the early days while leading worship one Sunday, I made a special effort to pay close attention to those who were standing and worshipping along with me, with their hands lifted without being asked or prompted to do so.

Over a period of about four weeks, I gathered these individuals together and shared with them my desire for them to be a part of this 'new' facet of ministry. After gathering about twelve individuals, I took one whole year to teach and pour into them the rudiments of Praise & Worship.

These individuals became our first praise team. I had the opportunity and pleasure to debut this team during a special service where all five of our congregations (*we had four morning services, in addition to a Sunday evening service*) gathered together to worship on the first Sunday of the year at the famed Shrine Auditorium in Los Angeles California.

I had to find a way to articulate and manifest the vision that Bishop Blake shared with me; the vision he had in his heart. And now, **that** vision, in large part has been realized – our people standing and lifting their hands in worship to the Father.

In 1990, West Angeles hosted its very first "See His Glory" Worship Symposium. Once again, something new was met with great resistance, but even the detractors could not deny the power and the overwhelming presence of God which not only filled the room, but also filled each longing heart!

As our Praise & Worship Team consecrated and sought the Lord for specifics on how the conference should be conducted, what workshops to present and who to invite to speak, it became evident that we were to lay out an unambiguous and concise blueprint, not only for the present, but also for posterity.

The purpose for these series of workshops over the years was clear: to further inculcate not only our congregation, but churches all over our nation with the revelation that we are to create a space for God to dwell through the vehicle of our praise which carries us to the destination of worship.

Spiritual luminaries such as the late Archbishop Wilbert S. McKinley of Brooklyn NY, the late Dr. Myles Monroe of Nassau Bahamas, the late Prophet Kim Clemment, of Detroit MI, Dr. Mark Hanby of Argyle TX, Bishop T.D. Jakes of Dallas, TX, Bishop Jacqueline McCullough of Brooklyn NY, Pastor Donnie McClurkin of Amityville, NY, Pastor Gary Oliver of Fort Worth, TX, and the list goes on; all of which came to assist us in the effort of lifting the awareness and consciousness of the people of God of the power in their worship.

As aforementioned, it was an arduous task to take on the assignment to shift the current culture to include and execute the vision in the heart of the leader, but what made it bearable was the frequent check ins, the mutual encouragement and laser focus on the goal which was to be achieved.

While each church setting is unique, the fact remains that the M.O.M. is responsible for effectively communicating and fulfilling the Pastor's expectations for the music ministry to those under their watch and finding ways to do so.

The "See His Glory" Worship Symposiums - three day conferences, our Worship Explosions – two day conferences, our Praise-A-Thon Shut-Ins – (*From 7:00 PM Friday evening to 7:00AM Saturday morning*), our Nights of Worship – Sunday Evening Services and our Wednesday Evening panel discussions on Worship, were all offshoots of the leadership's vision and were developed to further push the agenda of the vision.

The leader cannot achieve the vision alone. P.O.P. needs help! Through your ingenuity M.O.M., God will use your gifts and talents to assist your leader in actualizing the vision.

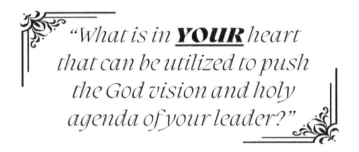

*"What is in **YOUR** heart that can be utilized to push the God vision and holy agenda of your leader?"*

Here is a question I would like to ask ....what is in **YOUR** heart that can be utilized to push the God vision and holy agenda of your leader? The fact that you are assigned to "that" house of worship, is an indicator that there is the discovery of something great which lies within you, postured to further the cause of the ministry right where you are; and, as you work on the dream(s) of others, God will work on yours!

This is not the time to give up, this is not the time to quit! No matter the difficulty, where you are is making you for your next! Yes - there will be times of frustration, disappointment and even doubting if God sent you there, but let me admonish you to hold on to the promises of God and work diligently as unto the Lord without murmuring or complaining.

Take it from me – the dividends are divine!

LOW HANGING FRUIT

When God gives a vision, it customarily seems as if the vision is diametrically opposed to our current reality. In these moments of waiting for the vision to manifest, it is important that we do not to allow substitutions to stand in the way or to become distractions to what God has promised.

Imagine this – P.O.P. has a plan for an initiative to guide the congregants toward inner transformation and personal empowerment, whose end goal is to help them awaken their true potential, cultivate compassion for others, and experience profound spiritual growth.

How does M.O.M. support this effort? By selecting material that speak to the theme and goal of the initiative.

I know the concept of marrying the music to the mandate seems very elementary and simplistic, but more often than not, M.O.M.s don't understand the importance of tying the song to the vision or goal of the P.O.P.

Sometimes M.O.M.s don't try hard enough; it is very easy to roll out of bed and do what we know to do because of the talent, gifting, and skill that many of us have acquired. I call this the low hanging fruit of the music ministry, not too much effort needed for the win. Let's discuss why it is necessary for us to avoid the low hanging fruit:

GOD DESERVES OUR BEST - We have all done it. Rushing through the week, procrastinating until the last possible moment to prepare material for the upcoming worship setting. Being so distracted during the week that our primary obligation is relegated to the back burner, then we find ourselves listening to the music for the first time in the car on the way to rehearsal.

This is Low Hanging Fruit!

God will only sit in the space that we carve out for Him and although in spite of our lack of preparation He blesses His people, we must never think that He was pleased with what we offered Him if it was less than our best.

We can decide to sing "I'm a soldier in the army of the Lord" and have the congregation clapping, singing, and dancing, but as it relates to our best, I ask this question. Did we deviate to that song because of our lack of preparation, or is that truly the message that needed to be conveyed in that worship setting?

When P.O.P.s vision goes beyond surface level practices or quick-fix solutions, avoiding the low hanging fruit means that the M.O.M. must do the same. In addition to the spiritual elements needed to fulfil the role, this also involves dedicating time to study, preparation and practice of execution because God deserves our best.

THOSE WE HAVE BEEN CALLED TO SERVE DESERVE OUR BEST - Avoiding the low hanging fruit translates to not shying away from bringing your best 'you' to the table. Those we serve are depending on us to lead them in a dimension of music ministry that will not only worship and honor God, lift the eyes of the congregation to see God, but lift them as well. When we arrive at any worship or rehearsal setting ill prepared and nonchalant, we silently shout that the team is not important and don't deserve the best we have to give. Those we are called to serve in any capacity, deserve our best.

YOU DESERVE YOUR BEST - As the M.O.M. - It is crucial to strive to be the best version of yourself, if for no one else but you!

Avoiding the low hanging fruit involves making choices that are in line with spiritual integrity, holding yourself to a higher standard than anyone else will. We must stretch and reach for the fruit on the branches on the tops of the trees. This takes great effort and determination, but what does that look like?

Studying your craft, bringing your "A" game to the table each time, every time, know your vocal parts, expand your worship vocabulary, *(I weary of worship leaders that can only say 'Hallelujah' and 'Let's praise the Lord' during a worship set)* ensuring that each part of your presentation is met with a level of excellence.

Recognizing that your vision involves aligning your life with spiritual principles and embracing all the practices that lead to distinction, it becomes essential to avoid settling for the easy or superficial.

Music Ministry is hard work, and you must be up to the task to make it happen. By doing so, you will embody the transformative power of music and inspire others through your commitment to spiritual depth and musical excellence.

NAVIGATING THE BALANCE BETWEEN TRADITION & INNOVATION

In my role as International Minister of Music for the Church of God in Christ, Inc., it was my aim to ensure that the musical offerings in each of our service settings possessed something for each generation. It was necessary to balance tradition with innovation and not allow either element to get in the way of the other.

Not all of our senior saints dislike the music of today, and not all young people dislike the music of their parents' generation. Navigating the balance between honoring the hymns and spirituals of old, and the music of today, takes wisdom and an understanding of each age group and the kind of musical presentation which speaks to them.

As a child, I grew up listening to my mother's favorite radio station (WFME Radio NY) which played classical music, choral anthems, hymns, a-capella and instrumental gospel music 24 hours a day. Every presentation was very well executed, a far cry from what was experienced at our church, where it was the responsibility of the deacons to lead at least four hymns a Sunday.

Some just made it through vocally, but all of them knew every stanza of those hymns. (*You know you are serious about the hymns when you call them stanzas and not verses!*)

As the result of hearing at least four to five hymns every Sunday for over twenty-one years, I learned and internalized the hymns; and now as an adult, I would dare to say that there are probably a handful of hymns that I do not know. Embracing the hymns provided a wonderful foundation for my overall approach to music ministry.

My introduction to the genre of Praise & Worship came upon my first year at ORU in the early eighties. Coming from a classic Pentecostal environment, I was enamored by what I encountered during my first chapel service at ORU. The students and faculty were all standing, hands lifted, many were dancing at will, which was so much different than what I had experienced growing up.

At the church of my childhood, the spirit had to "hit" you in order for you to dance, and if it didn't and you decided to dance, you were sat down by the mothers of the church, because it was looked upon as if you were playing with God. To see thousands of individuals dancing "at will" for me was a bit strange, but I was certainly intrigued by it.

I had the sense that this thing called 'Praise & Worship' was something the Lord wanted me to engage in, but I just did not know how.

Shortly thereafter, I joined a church on the Northside of Tulsa, aptly named – Northside Christian Center COGIC. It was here that I was exposed to the late Dr. Myles Monroe of Nassau, Bahamas. I remember it like it was yesterday because that Sunday in April of 1986 changed my life forever!

The service started promptly at 3:00 pm. Not many people attended this particular service, but Dr. Monroe was preaching and teaching like there were thousands of people in the room. That evening, he taught on the Seven Hebrew words for Praise. I had never heard anything like the revelation that was pouring from his lips.

I took copious notes and upon return to my apartment that evening, began a very deep dive into what I had just learned.

In those days, we did not have the convenience of the internet to quickly research a topic, all I had was my Strong's Concordance my Bible dictionary and a writing tablet. For the next four weeks, I studied and ingested all I could about Praise and Worship.

As I matriculated through ORU, my understanding of what Worship was intensified and I grew to understand that praise is a vehicle, but our worship is the destination - the culmination or zenith of our praise.

The vehicle may be beautiful and an enjoyable means for traveling the road; but when we get to the destination of worship, we must not dwell in the vehicle. We must get out of the vehicle and go to the destination that prompted our travel in the first place.

Navigating the balance between tradition and innovation is a difficult task, which must be met with prayer, council, wisdom, and strategy. The vehicles of one generation will not be as shiny and new as the vehicles of others, but both must be respected, appreciated and are necessary to get the respective generation to the destination of worship.

Song medleys were one of the means by which the congregation was taught to appreciate the 'vehicle' in the early days of the praise and worship movement in the early 90s'. We would start out by singing a very familiar congregational song, and after we sang it so much that the congregation was on their feet, rejoicing and praising God, we shifted to include a new song comprising the same key and beat.

Although unfamiliar with the new song, the congregation joined in after the worship team sang about three rounds of the song. (*This was before the luxury of having the words on the screens*) The congregation participated because they were already on their feet enjoying what they previously heard and after they got to the place where they enjoyed that song in the middle, we switched back to the original familiar song. The congregation loved it!

The following Sunday, the worship set started out with the song, which was previously unfamiliar, then introducing a brand new song, finally closing out with the song we started with. We continued this "sandwich" method for several months until we introduced quite a number of new songs to the congregation. They learned the songs because we started with what was familiar to them, and then brought them on a journey with us in being exposed to new songs of praise to the Lord.

This medley concept as well as other means of educating the congregation were initiated after coming to the realization that P.O.P and M.O.M.s understanding of the vehicle to worship and the road to get there was not readily comprehended by everyone, and a rejection of what we were trying to convey was not taken personally, but was utilized as a challenge to overcome, as opposed to a roadblock to stop progress.

M.O.M., if you have been called to navigate the waters of shifting a mindset and culture, I encourage you to do so with patience and grace. Keep moving. If you have the approval of P.O.P, keep innovation as a handy tool in your arsenal. If the agenda before you is God's agenda, He will watch over His word to perform it as you use your creatively to synergize the old and the new – thus bridging the gap.

> *"If you have been called to navigate the waters of shifting a mindset and culture, I encourage you to do so with patience and grace."*

SELAH

CHAPTER THREE

PRACTICAL APPLICATIONS

In this section of the book, I offer a few suggestions for practical application of the aforementioned principles to assist you in your quest to understand the cohesive nature that must exist in order for the relationship between MOM and POP to thrive. It's good to know what to do, but even better to know how to do what needs to be done.

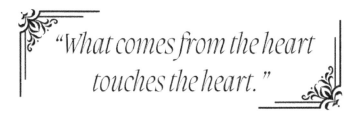

"What comes from the heart touches the heart."

There is a saying I often use when instructing those in the music ministry about the transparency needed to connect their audience to the authenticity of the worship moment; "What comes from the heart touches the heart". The congregation can discern phoniness and pretense miles away!

It is important for those who stand before the congregation, to do so from an authentic place. As yoke fellows in the ministry, M.O.M. and P.O.P. must be able to synergize and minister together from the heart.

Since the function of the Minister of Music is given to support the vision of the Pastor, it is important for the M.O.M. to learn the heart of the P.O.P.

LEARN THE HEART

1 Thessalonians 5:12 says:

> *And we beseech you, brethren, to know them which labor among you, and* **are over you in the Lord**, *and admonish you;* **And to esteem them very highly in love for their work's sake.** *And be at peace among yourselves.*

I recently received a powerful revelation on this scripture. We often quote the first part of the verse, but often fail to read on and as a result, miss a very important message from the passage. "Know those who labor among you **AND** are over you in the Lord and admonish you...."

We are commanded not only to know our fellow soldiers on the battlefield, but to also to know our leaders, know their heart, know their proverbial cadence, know how they "roll".

Note also that this scripture admonishes us to esteem those who are over us "very highly in love for their work's sake..." I view this portion of the verse from this standpoint; if there is a high regard for the leader, then those serving with them will attempt to do what is necessary to lift the load of the leader in any way possible.

For an example, let's take a look at a story in the Bible which allows us the opportunity to lean into this principle.

Exodus 17:11 & 12

11 And it came to pass, when Moses held up his hand, that Israel prevailed: and when he let down his hand, Amalek prevailed. 12 But Moses hands were heavy; and they took a stone, and put it under him, and he sat thereon; and Aaron and Hur stayed up his hands, the one on the one side, and the other on the other side; and his hands were steady until the going down of the sun.

Here, we are brought into the narrative where Moses becomes fatigued due to the day long battle against the Amalekites. Even in his fatigue, note that the scripture does not give us any indication that Moses asked for rest or assistance.

There are times when the leader does not know what they need or how to obtain what they need, and it's in those moments that those who support the leader should take on the spirit of Aaron and Hur, whose ingenuity kicked in to find a solution to the problem at hand.

They provided rest with the rock and assistance by holding up their leaders' arms.

As a side note, sometimes all a leader needs are rest and some assistance with the burden of leadership. M.O.M., fulfill your role in assisting in the area to which you have been assigned. Watch how God will bless you for being the one who thinks ahead and suggests solutions to ease the load of the P.O.P.

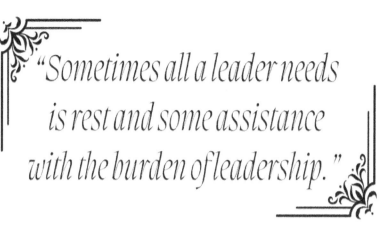

"Sometimes all a leader needs
is rest and some assistance
with the burden of leadership."

Aaron and Hur had to know the heart of their leader.
They had to have some knowledge of how Moses
would respond to their actions and have been
comfortable enough to engage and move forward with
their plan.

Similarly, Moses had to know the hearts of Aaron and
Hur and have confidence that what they were
proposing to do came from a place of love, care, and
concern as opposed to usurping authority and
dictating to Moses what was going to happen and how
it was going to happen. From this observation we note
that there must be mutual trust.

In addition, it is extremely important that P.O.P.
knows that they are held in high regard by M.O.M.
The level of respect and encouragement from those
who serve under the leader is important, especially for
the battle-weary leader.

Here are some pointers.

- <u>Close observation of the Pastor,</u> listening intently to what is said and subsequently what is not said, will aid and assist the M.O.M. in learning the heart of the P.O.P.

A wise M.O.M. will observe the Pastor's responses to the music offered during services and base future repertoire choices on the genre that invokes their most passionate worship.

- The music ministry must <u>prepare the congregation to receive</u> the Pastor's message. Remember that the ministry of music is the tool used to till (excavate, dig) the ground, to prepare the soil (the hearts of the congregation) for the seed (the Word of God).

The music should direct the focus Godward and bring the congregation into a place in worship where they are ready to receive the Word.

There should never be a time when the Pastor has to till the ground **AND** deliver the seed. The pastor should not have to motivate the congregation to worship after the music ministry has done so.

However, it is the Pastor's prerogative to do so if they wish, but not on account of the deficit created by the lack of preparation on the part of the music ministry.

The hearts of the people should be so prepared by the time the music ministry has concluded that they are waiting with anticipation, hungering, and thirsting for the Word of God

- **The M.O.M. should intercede for the Pastor during the delivery of the sermon**. Be mindful that the enemy attempts to bring thoughts of doubt and despair while he/she is preaching with things like, *"This is not working...People are not growing....You are inadequate..... Why don't you just shut up and sit down? This is a waste of your time and theirs.... Nobody wants to hear you...."*
Because of the mental warfare that is prone to engage during this time of ministry, it is a very precious source of encouragement when a Pastor knows that someone is praying for them while they minister.

A Minister of Music should become so well acquainted with the heart and vision of the Pastor that constant interfacing is not a dire necessity. However, this ability to walk in tandem without always being in the "face" of the leader comes only after a length of time, testing and trust.

The Minister of Music should endeavor to develop an amount of trust and understanding, to a level that allows him to stay out of the Pastor's way and simply complete the tasks that have been assigned.

A PERSONAL EXPERIENCE

Each time Bishop Blake spoke, I made it a point to take notes. I attempted to be at every general meeting outside of the worship moment on Sundays and mid-week Bible study to hear my leader. As I reviewed the notes and recalled what was spoken, I began to develop an understanding of what it was he desired. In those general meetings, he almost never spoke directly to what he desired in the Music Department, but I took the principles he shared in other areas and asked the Lord for wisdom to apply them to the Music Ministry.

It took a few years, but after a while, because my staff and I had studied Bishop Blake and knew where his heart was concerning ministry and the things of God, if he shared with me something he would like to have done, it would never fail that my staff and I were already into the planning of that thing.

We were in sync!

Allow me to share with you one experience to highlight this model.

The Holy Days on the Christian calendar come every year, and the M.O.M. should allot a significant amount of time – nine month **minimum** – for planning for the special Holy Days.

About four years after becoming the Minister of Music, I wanted to do something special for the Christmas services, because that year, Christmas actually fell on a Sunday. West Angeles had a history of spectacular Christmas presentations, but this year, I wanted to do something a bit different, so I gathered a group of singers that knew how to read music, contracted out a small orchestra, had a designer to create formal tuxedo outfits for the choir, and on that Christmas Sunday, after three months of weekly sectional rehearsals, on Tuesdays and Thursdays, combined rehearsals on Saturdays, we performed for all four of our morning services, "For Unto us A Child Is Born" and "The Hallelujah Chorus" from the Handel's Messiah.

When Bishop Blake walked into the pulpit, for the 7:00 AM service, his face lit up and he smiled from ear to ear. This was something that had been in his heart, but we never discussed it – he never told me. I simply put into practice what I heard him say in other settings –

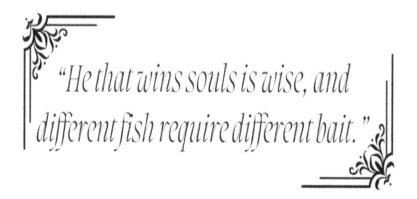

"He that wins souls is wise, and different fish require different bait."

"The people who attend our church are multidimensional, and we must ensure that our ministry is attractive; that it reaches and touches every aspect of who our people are. I would like our ministry to be like a supermarket, that people can come and find anything they may need. He that wins souls is wise and different fish require different bait."

We heard you Bishop!

This one concept has kept me on a quest to ensure that my ministry is never pigeonholed into one idiom, expression, or sound. The music in heaven is resplendent with variety, all of it holy, but diverse, nonetheless. Because I have an awareness of this, my prayer is: "Lord your Kingdom come, and your will be done **IN** earth as it is in heaven!"

INFORMATION IS KEY

Now I know that this particular heading may seem like a paradox and contradiction, given what I just explained was my experience, but you will note that I also stated that it took a number of years for the relational trust to be established.

TRUST is the key factor which allows the MOM to have the latitude to move within the sphere of responsibility as assigned.

Until that trust is developed, a pastor should know what is going on in his/her church and the Minister of Music must develop and execute a strategy which facilitates clear, concise communication.

The Pastor should always be informed of:

Departmental Goals And Events - No activities should be commenced without pastoral approval. Reports and **written proposals** provide one method for achieving this. Given that the M.O.M. is a creative, there are often times when great ideas will come at the spur of the moment. In those moments (*I have done this*) the propensity can be to run with that idea without examining the pros and cons. The practice of delivering a weekly checklist of items which included as much information regarding that particular idea, and how it will impact not only my area of responsibility, but the potential impact to other areas of the church, became a necessity. All decisions made create a ripple effect that have impact on the entire body.

The Agenda For Each Worship Service – In the early 90's, before Planning Center became a mainstream online service planning software (*one which I highly recommend you utilize if you are not already*) I prepared what I called an *"FYI Sheet"* each week for leadership, and everyone involved in the worship aspect of the services. This document was delivered each Friday and provided a snapshot of what was proposed to take place during the Sunday worship service, e.g., the ministering choir, the song selection, attendance of special guests, etc. This document became a necessity, because it provided the necessary information to connect the dots so everyone would be on the same sentence on the page.

The Temperature Of The "House" – In the natural, because of proximity, the Mother will usually be the one to have conversations with the children about what is going on with them and what they are looking forward to in the future.

When my children were much younger, they would come to me with what they wanted prior to going to their Dad. They did this often because they wanted to feel me out to see what I was going to say before they approached their Dad.

Then, there were other times when they would feel more comfortable coming to me with issues and problems they were experiencing, not because they did not trust their Dad, but there is something about being able to talk to "Momma". Now if it was not a weighty matter that I expressed to them that they needed to tell him, I would share with him what was going on in the house.

Those in the Levitical arena will usually express to the M.O.M. what they are feeling and their observation of the ministry from where they stand. (*Side note – the spiritual purpose of the platform is to be aware of what is going on in the room, to minister and pray to the end that God has his way in the service).* It is the M.O.M.'s responsibility to truthfully communicate these things to the P.O.P. and offer suggestions as to how any issue may be mitigated.

COLLABORATION AND COMMUNICATION

Effective communication is a weapon which can combat many of the forces that seek to destroy a relationship. The Minister of Music who desires to maintain a clear channel of communication with their Pastor should do the following:

ESTABLISH A REGULAR MEETING SCHEDULE

During these meetings, the M.O.M. will have the opportunity to:

- *Share plans with the Pastor; and be as detailed as possible.* Keep the Pastor updated on activities, planned events and new ideas. What are the pros and cons? When and where will it take place? Who are the participants? The P.O.P. should know what is going on in your area of responsibility.

- *Remember that a relationship of trust is the foundation for having difficult conversations.*

I am frequently asked, "How do I tell my Pastor the things that I don't want to say, even though I know that I need to say them?"

A relationship of trust will facilitate the P.O.P.'s willingness and openness to receive truth, and the M.O.M. must be led by the Spirit of God regarding when and how certain items are addressed.

Sensitive issues must never be proclaimed before a crowd. Not only will the P.O.P. reject what has been spoken, but it will bring a breach in relationship, and loss of trust.

Since trust is earned and takes time to develop, it is precious and must be handled very delicately, since it is needed in order to operate a successful working relationship between M.O.M. and P.O.P.

> "Trust is earned and takes time to develop, it is precious and must be handled very delicately."

Be proactive in the sharing of information

-   *Share honest feelings because honesty is always the best policy.* When asked, the M.O.M. should be truthful in expressing his/her perspective on issues. If an opinion has not been solicited, it should still be expressed, but in a respectful manner. Open and honest communication with the Minister of Music will give the P.O.P. the assurance needed to trust and feel at ease when important decisions regarding the music ministry must be made.

-   *If you see something, say something.* P.O.P. may not always know what is going on in the "household", so if the M.O.M. sees a potential issue arising, it is incumbent on them to share with P.O.P. what the cause for concern is.

Seek input and feedback

-   Evaluations are important, they help the M.O.M. to stay on track. After you have completed your own self-evaluation, share with the P.O.P. your findings, and ask for input and feedback regarding what you have accessed.
    Be open to receive what you may not want to hear, because M.O.M. sometimes can veer off course, albeit with good intentions, but needs to be brought back into alignment with the direction, purpose, and vision of the house.

- M.O.M., if P.O.P. only sees you when it is time to 'shine', that is a problem. Actively participating in events outside of the formal responsibility of music ministry allows the people to whom you minister each week, the opportunity to know and fellowship with you. This practice also builds a level of trust between you and those with whom you fellowship; and although extracurricular church events may not be mandatory, the staff meetings and active participation in them should be compulsory.

PRAYER AND ENCOURAGEMENT

A Minister of Music must intercede and pray for the P.O.P. They need encouragement. They need to know that they are supported, appreciated, and remembered in prayer. It means a lot to hear "I am praying for you, God bless you, I am in your corner." Compared to compliments, a Pastor hears so many more complaints.

There are many challenges that he/she must deal with, while still being expected to exemplify strength, poise, and cordiality. As saints, we must realize that our pastors, ministers, and elders are human; and they need to hear "Whatever you need, Pastor, I'm there."

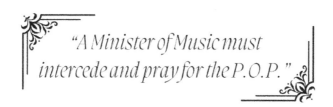

"A Minister of Music must intercede and pray for the P.O.P."

The M.O.M. has been called to support the Pastor not only when everyone is looking, but also while at home, lifting up the ministry of the Pastor and the ministry of the church in prayer.

Several years ago, the Lord led our Praise & Worship team to pray specifically, in a concentrated season of prayer for Bishop Blake and Lady Mae. We fasted every Wednesday and, for the first four months of that year, we prayed earnestly for them as a group. We even put it on our monthly ministry calendar to keep it before us. I shared with him one day what we were doing, and he was grateful that we were sensitive to the Lord and taken the initiative to pray for he and Lady Mae in that manner.

You can imagine how preaching four morning services and often the evening service on Sundays, in addition to all of the traveling he would do during the week would wear on one's body, so we prayed that the strength of the Lord would continue to sustain, uphold, and undergird him with the anointing and fortitude to carry out each and every assignment, with the anointing, effectiveness and excellence.

Encouragement in word and deed, coupled with prayer, are principles that should be practiced as they contribute to the maintenance of a healthy relationship between M.O.M. and P.O.P.

LOYALTY

The Pastoral journey is often a lonely road.

Being a PK (Preacher's Kid) afforded me the opportunity to observe firsthand, just how lonely a road pastoring a people can be. Being a Pastor often entails taking on the burdens and challenges of others which can certainly be draining and isolating. Pastors are expected to provide encouragement, support, and guidance to their parishioners at all times, but may not always receive the same level of support or encouragement in return.

The faithfulness and loyalty of those who have been brought close in ministry, can be a great source of encouragement and support. When issues or problems that occur within the church are unnecessarily spread, the pastor can become wounded.

Pastors, like all of us, are human; and they face the same emotions we all experience.

If they have spent time grooming, caring for and imparting into a group of individuals, it is hurtful to hear of disloyalty among them or discovering that they are the catalyst for drama within the church.

The expectations placed on Pastors can be very demanding, and this can create a sense of pressure and the need to always be "on".

P.O.P, one of M.O.M.'s most underutilized postures of loyalty is the sensitivity and perceptivity they possess to be aware of the leader's load. This particular posture of loyalty is concerned about the general well-being of the P.O.P. and indicates the ability to take problems away from the leader and solve them within their given sphere of responsibility and influence.

Moreover, loyalty does not only encompass the aspect of 'being present', with boots on the ground, but also what transpires when one is not in the physical vicinity of the person to whom we have been assigned. The internal dialogue as well as the external, should glorify the Lord.

In many cases, it is easier said than done, especially when there are misunderstandings or there has been mistreatment of any kind. In these cases, we are not responsible for what happens to us, we are however, responsible for our response to **what** has transpired.

There are indeed times when we must speak up for ourselves or speak to the situation as we view it, but then there are times when through prayer and meditation the instruction will come, " Hold your peace". I am a witness that the Lord's way is always best.

True loyalty to a person and the assignment indicates an understanding of the divine mission and is not necessarily centered around and/or dependent on monetary gain. The M.O.M. who vacates a current assignment to run after the highest dollar in another location, not only operates in a spirit which does not trust God to provide for their needs in the current place of assignment, but also boarders on taking on the personification of a hireling.

Conversely, the leader who says to an individual in another man's vineyard: "If you come to my church, I'll pay you this amount of money" fails to consider that it will only be a matter of time before they will face the same experience. *"Be not deceived; God is not mocked: for whatsoever a man soweth, that shall he also reap."(Galatians 6:7, KJV)*

Consider this scenario: Music minister X is unhappy in his current ministry assignment, the people are getting on his nerves, the Pastor won't give him more freedom and control, etc. Pastor Y from another church notices the frustration of Minister X and offers him $50,000 more to come to his church. Minister X accepts the offer and leaves, without the blessing of Pastor Y.

What Music Minister X does not realize is that, after a period of time, he will be the same frustrated, dissatisfied person who left the first assignment. We must reach a level of spiritual maturity, accountability, and stability, understanding that our experiences are not about what is being done **TO** us, but they are God's tools to work things **OUT** of us and develop character **IN** us.

There will be no lasting fulfillment for those who abandon their place of assignment and run from God's process of development.

Having said that, let me state this. Ministers of Music (*musicians, choir directors, worship leaders, etc.*) should be compensated at a level commensurate with the churches' ability to provide for them.

Can I hear the Ministers of Music shout **AMEN!**

These areas of ministry within the church are synonymous with the biblical Levitical order, who were sustained by what was received from the temple. (1 Samuel 2: 13&14)

The posture I have personally seen some leaders take of "These musicians should do it for free, because God gave them the gift for free", is unbiblical and harmful.

Deuteronomy 25:4 –
> *"Thou shalt not muzzle the ox when he treadeth out the corn."*

This passage commands that anyone working to accomplish a task with some degree of intentionality, should not be deferred from enjoying a part of that which was produces by their labor.

Yes – Even the musicians!

Now – allow me to bring balance. If the M.O.M., or musician, has to utilize the transpose button to play in every key, if the choir director is always late for rehearsals and services, if the worship leader takes no care to learn the material until they arrive to rehearsal, If the choir director arrives to the church disheveled and smelling like weed, then another decision needs to be made!!

That kind of behavior must not be tolerated, even if they are the most talented musicians in the city. God's house deserves the very best, anointed, skillful, dedicated, and loyal Levities.

SELAH

CHAPTER FOUR

POSITIVE RESULTS

THE IMPACT OF UNITY

"Behold, how good and how pleasant it is for brethren to dwell
together in unity - for there the LORD **commanded** *the*
blessing even life for evermore"
(Psalm 133:1,3 – KJV, emphasis added)

Why is the relationship between Pastor and Minister of Music so vital? It's because the blessing of God is guaranteed in an environment of unity. When M.O.M. and P.O.P. walk in sync together, God's commanded blessing causes all things which are out of line to come into alignment; and areas which present challenges will be positively impacted:

> • **Giving** – If God commands His blessing on a church, the people will gladly support its mission.

> • **Attendance** – If God's blessing is on the house, His glory will abide; and the people will faithfully attend because they want to be there.

> • **Service** – The blessing of unity will cause believers to walk in faithfulness to their individual calls to ministry; and their gifts will assist the church in areas where their talents are needed.

• **Relationships** – An environment of unity will diminish negativity to promote an atmosphere of love and support among parishioners.

• **Fellowship with other churches** – The Pastor who trusts his M.O.M. - confident that they will not be "stolen" by another Pastor - will not hesitate to join forces with other Pastors and/or allow his M.O.M. to minister outside of his home church.

UNDERSTANDING
THE ASSIGNMENT

What about the M.O.M. who abides by the principles expressed in Chapter 1, but serves in a house and with a POP whose mindset presents a true hindrance to impactful ministry?

Obviously, hardship is much easier to bear if it's only for a season, and in this, the M.O.M must not abdicate their role due to the difficulty but must understand the assignment and the greater true value of their function, remaining steadfast to what has been given into their charge. What in essence has God called you to do? When God gives an assignment, it is incumbent upon us to complete the assignment and to do so with excellence.

Having served as the International Minister of Music and President of the International Music Department of the Church of God in Christ for a total of 12 years, I had the awesome opportunity to travel the length and breadth of this country and around the world, visiting churches within our denomination as well as without. All churches are not blessed to have a situation where the Pastor was a musician, who understood the spiritual and creative process necessary for the Minister of Music to produce excellence on a consistent basis.

In addition to numerous attributes I appreciate about Bishop Charles E. Blake, Sr., is that once he communicated what it was he desired to see, he left it to me to make it happen. He believed in the adage – "Let the people that do the job, do the job!" If there was an instance where he needed to correct me (*and there were quite a few* -), he never did it publicly, or embarrass me in his presence. He understood that the people sent to him by God were gifts to assist him in advancing the Kingdom and he allowed us to operate in our gifting and in our call.

In my travels, I observed quite a few leaders who felt as if they had to do it all. This mindset is never good. As aforementioned, God has called workers to assist the vision and if the Pastor continues to push the people away by attempting to do it all, the vision will not be realized.

Proverbs 29:18a states – "Where there is no vision, the people perish...", but consequently, where there are no people, the vision will perish. Leaders who try to do it all will find themselves burnt out, frustrated and ultimately, not able to fulfill the assignment.

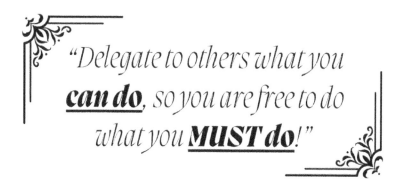

*"Delegate to others what you **can do**, so you are free to do what you **MUST do**!"*

Quite a few years ago while feverishly preparing for the Holy Convocation of the Church Of God In Christ, the Lord spoke very clearly to me and said,

> *"I indeed have anointed and equipped you with the ability to accomplish and do many things well, but, in this season daughter, you **MUST** delegate to others what you **can do**, so you are free to do what you **MUST do**!"*

This word from the Lord shook me to my core and came at a time when I was in the midst of restructuring my staff for the next quadrennial of leadership. I heeded the Word from the Lord and strategically delegated everything I could, to dozens of trusted individuals.

Needless to say, that Convocation was one of the best that I had personally experienced in my leadership up until that point, due in part, to the fact that I allowed my staff to carry the vision of our department, a music department that would not know only how to sing, how to dance and shout, but a holy army of Levites who understood their responsibility, through the anointing, through order and organization, how to "Set the Atmosphere, Protect the Atmosphere and Maintain the Atmosphere".

I had to let go, to gain. In so doing, not only was I able to enjoy the Convocation, (*The Levites work from Sun-up to Sun-up!*) but I was able to see the fruits of my labor by observing those who I poured into, flourish and execute their responsibility with a great dimension of excellence and the anointing. By attempting to do it all I was in essence preventing others from their opportunity to grow and thrive.

Leaders who feel like they need to do it all, micromanaging every step, are often unaware of the revelation that God has placed resources in individuals around that them who will assist in advancing the work.

Leaders who do not allow **trusted, qualified, and proficient** staff a certain level of anonymity to operate within their sphere of responsibility and assignment without having to ask for approval for **every** decision within their area, will soon find themselves in a real quandary; burnt out, depressed, and often times adopting ungodly coping mechanisms to anesthetize the weight of the burden.

Conversely, it is just as burdensome for a leader to experience the frustration of working with those who have been assigned to assist, but in turn actually bring more work to the leader by not operating at the level of excellence which is desired by the leader.

Time is of the essence, and if a leader must themselves repeat a task because it was done in a manner which could be detrimental to the entire operation, that constitutes a problem which must be addressed and rectified.

It is extremely important for those who have been selected to assist leadership understand their role and embrace the responsibility of lifting the leader, as opposed to causing them stress and strain.

EVERYTHING YOU NEED IS IN THE HOUSE

Leaders – God has placed everything you need to accomplish your goal, desire, and dream within your reach!

In 2 Kings chapter 4, we read the account of a widow woman who cried out to the prophet Elisha at the point of desperation, because the creditors were coming to take her sons (her future) to pay off a tremendous debt.

Elisha asked her two questions in verse 2
>"…. What shall I do for thee? tell me, what hast thou in the house?"

She responded
>"Thine handmaid hath not anything in the house, save a **pot of oil**."

Nothing – **BUT** a pot of oil…..!

All she needed was already in the house, she just needed to be made aware of what it was she possessed, how to make room for it, and how to active it so that her present needs and the posterity of her future would be secure.

Similarly, God has placed what is needed for the "house" in each "house", which is often overlooked and considered too insignificant to remedy the problem at hand, as referenced by the response of the widow woman. If the pot of oil could talk, it would say something like this:

"I am here in the corner; all I need is an opportunity to grow and all you need is locked up in what God has given me to be to you. I am here to assist you. Just pour me in a few jars and watch what will happen."

It is the ultimately responsibility of the leader to ascertain what is "in the house" and utilize it for the good of the house and ultimately, the Kingdom!"

What is a M.O.M. to do if they are faced with a leader who is not aware of what is "in the house"; the gifts and talents available to assist in the glorification of God, the evangelization of the world and the edification of believers? How are they to posture themselves in this type of environment?

That Minister of Music should:

Reconnect with "The Assignment" - Once again – communication is key. Share what you perceive to be the skills and giftings you have that will assist in achieving the vision; and ask for an assessment of what has transpired thus far in the carrying out the vision.

Ask the Pastor questions similar to the following: How do you feel I am doing with achieving what you have shared within your heart concerning the Music Ministry? What can I do to assist in a greater capacity?

Questions such as these create the opportunity for deeper dialogue and discussion. The M.O.M. must seek the Lord for clarity and not approach this time with pre-conceived notions as to what will be said or perceived by P.O.P.

Understand the "Timing of God" –
I wish to deal with this in three aspects.

ASPECT ONE - God has a divine purpose and timing for that purpose to be brought into manifestation. Waiting on God, for a person who is a creative, is often a challenge because of the impulsive manner by which most creatives operate.

We are often impatient with the process.

Trusting the timing of God will exemplify faith which sees the unknown process, and yet decides to go through it. Hebrews 12:2 – Looking unto Jesus the author and finisher of our faith, who for the joy that was set before him, endured the cross, despising the shame, and is set down at the right hand of the throne of God. Jesus saw the glorious end but went through process. We in like fashion, must do the same.

The creative element of the M.O.M. will often produce ideas or plans for which the P.O.P. is not quite ready for. This does not mean that God didn't give it. It just means that *"To everything there is a season, and a time to every purpose under the heaven"*.(Ecclesiastes 3:1). Timing is very important!

Much of what I am walking and operating in today, was birthed many years ago in the furnaces of trial and affliction. Coming through and out of those seasons, I mistakenly assumed that I would be released to immediately implement what God had revealed to me in the past, about my future. How frustrated and sad I was to discover that although I saw the zenith of the promise, there were greater hurdles and mountains which had to be conquered; and the process was not "over". It would only be through and in God's divine timing, in "the fullness of time" that it would all make sense. *Whatever the Holy Ghost gives will keep until the appointed time.*

ASPECT TWO - The M.O.M.'s focus during difficult circumstances should not be directed in great respect toward what is being endured; but rather, focused on how we respond to the circumstances.

The key questions are - 'What is God trying to teach me?", "What is He showing me about myself?" You may have been treated in an ill manner; and in no way am I suggesting that the ill treatment is right or to be excused.

However, one must focus on the fact that every circumstance gives us an opportunity to learn and grow. Take the time to reflect and consider: "What lesson am I to learn from this?" How is God using this situation to process me for my 'next'?

Here is an acronym to assist with your maintenance of proper **FOCUS:**

F – **Faith**   Stay committed to the process and believe that God, despite what you see, will keep his promises to you. (2 Corinthians 1:20)

O – **Obey**   The Scripture declares in Jeremiah 7:23 – "Obey my voice, and I will be your God, and ye shall be my people: and walk ye in all the ways that I have commanded you, that it may be well unto you."

C – **Connect**   Pray about and seek out individuals who are on the same spiritual path, to engage in prayer and methods of mutual support and encouragement. (Ecclesiastes 4: 9&10)

U – **Unify**   Be the one to transcend division. Seek peace and pursue it. (Psalm 133:1-3)

S – **See**   The right prescription in a pair of glasses will allow one to FOCUS and see clearly. Your **perspective** will aid in your success or failure. See yourself as the overcomer that you are. Visualize better – for "what you see, is what you be…" (Proverbs 29:18)

ASPECT THREE - Understand The Purpose Of Process. When I think of the word 'process', I am reminded of what a shofar has to go through to become a useful instrument in the hand of the priest.

<u>There is a sound that God is looking for in the earth</u>; and when that sound and frequency are achieved, it creates an atmosphere conducive for receiving the best that God desires to give to us. Often that sound is crafted through the hard times, times where one would have the propensity to give up or throw in the proverbial towel.

God is not trying to kill you. He wants to make you a vessel in His hands to sound an alarm, heralding His goodness to His people, and declaring salvation to a generation not cognizant of His power and might.

The making of a shofar includes the completion of a vigorous process to become a useful vessel. First, the horn of the ram is cut away from its' head, then the horn is boiled in hot water for a few hours.

Either a wooden or brass extraction instrument, (reminiscent of a long ice pick) is inserted into the horn with the intention of removing the flesh and cartilage which was not readily removed by being submerged and boiled in the hot water.

After all the visible flesh and cartilage is removed, the horn is once again placed in boiling water to remove the remnants of what the first dip and extraction did not remove. Following this process, it is placed on a shelf to cool and to dry.

Once dried, the tip of the horn is cut away and it is then placed in a vat of hot oil - not once, not twice, but three times, with a period of a few hours between each trip to the hot oil.

You Are Being Hollowed Out To Produce God's Sound

Just as a ram's horn undergoes a rigorous process to become a shofar, those who are called to 'sound the trumpet' must go through seasons of processing in order to become God's instruments through which His voice can be heard.

We ought not be surprised by the 'heat' and pressure we face. The focal point and purpose of the process is to make us pliable in the Master's hands, bringing us to a point of complete submission to His will and purpose.

The trials we face function as the pick and drill, cutting away the carnality within and leaving a holy, hollowed vessel through which God can speak clearly.

Psalm 62:11 King James Version (KJV)

> "God hath spoken once; twice have I heard this; that power belonged unto God."

Allow me to pose a question ... how can a voice spoken once, be heard twice?

AN ECHO!

An echo is produced and derived from an area that is empty and clean…much like that shofar.

Be encouraged M.O.M. To be perfected is the purpose of the process, for the Father to be able to speak through your life - enabling others to hear the proclamation of God's love and goodness

Let's Pause to Pray -

Lord, here we are as Your vessels. Dig us out! We ask that You remove those things that would hinder our forward movement in You. Remove those areas Father, that have held us in captivity, that have held us down for years, and years, and years.

Remove those areas in us causing fear, low self-esteem, pride, arrogance, apprehension, anything not like You, which would cause us not to be faithful, steadfast, unmovable, and always abounding in Your work.

Father, we release these things to You today, We surrender! We say 'Yes' to You, and yield all to Your Spirit to have Your way in us! In Jesus Mighty and matchless name, we pray – AMEN!

SELAH

Feel free to write on this page how
Chapter Four spoke to you.

CHAPTER FIVE

NECESSARY TOOLS

PERSONAL DEVOTION

May the life that I live reflect Your glory,
May the words that I speak honor Your name,
May the thoughts that I think be pleasing unto You,
May my life be a praise unto You Lord.

A lifestyle of worship to fulfill Your holy purpose,
To be pleasing and acceptable in Your sight,
Nothing else can compare to living in Your perfect will,
May my life be a praise unto You Lord!

These words are from a song I penned entitled "A Lifestyle of Worship", which speaks the sentiments of my heart; that everything I am, will bring honor unto His name. Ask yourself. What does a lifestyle of worship look like? M.O.M., worship is more than what we do, it is who we are. Our lives ought to reflect the very essence of the nature and presence of God. Easier said than done?

YES!!!

However, each day we should endeavor to *"grow in grace and in the knowledge of our Lord and Savior Jesus Christ."* (2 Peter 3:18) and *"press toward the mark of the high calling of God in Jesus Christ."* (Philippians 3:14)

It is important for M.O.M. to have a life of consistent personal devotion to stay rooted and grounded in the purpose for which we exist. It is so easy to fall prey to the Lucifer mentality if we don't.

PRAYER

A life of Prayer is vital for the success of anyone who is endeavoring to undertake any aspect of ministry, and the same holds true for the one who wishes to engage in Levitical artistry.

The power of prayer, coupled with the discipline of fasting empowers the individual to navigate and execute in the spirit realm with authority and accuracy.

I have personally found it quite difficult at times to maintain that 'perfect place' of prayer, even though I know it is something that I must live by. Life, and the cares of the world, can often creep in to dislodge us from the place where we are empowered – PRAYER.

M.O.M, as the one who is responsible for leading your team in *"Setting the Atmosphere, Maintaining the Atmosphere and Protecting the Atmosphere"*, you must make prayer an absolute priority in your life. Our gifting and skill to execute our craft, are necessary components, but will only take us so far. That which is needful is most important.

In Luke chapter 10 verses 38-42, we read the account of Martha extending hospitality to Jesus after arriving in their village.

Martha had a sister named Mary, who decided to be in the presence of Jesus, as opposed to assisting Martha at that moment. Martha was upset and complained to Jesus about it, but Jesus answered her and said:

> *"Martha, Martha, thou art careful and troubled about many things: But one thing is needful: and Mary hath chosen **that good part,** which shall not be taken away from her."* (Luke 10:41,42)

You see, Martha's role of providing hospitality to Jesus was a needed responsibility, however, Mary chose the good part; the part of sitting at the feet of Jesus.

In a proverbial sense, both the qualities of Mary and Martha are needful to accomplish any spiritual aspiration, however, there must be a balance between the two.

> *"There are times when working 'for' God can so busy us, that we remove ourselves from being 'before' God."*

There are times when working 'for' God, can so busy us, that we remove ourselves from being 'before' God.

I am sure that all of us can attest to the overwhelming aspects of life, which at times keep us from being intimate with the Lord in prayer, and in those times, I have personally found it necessary to ensure that I engaged in a strategy that would assist me in maintaining my focus and causing my passion for His presence to be fully realized.

What is a strategy?

A strategy involves setting goals, determining actions to achieve the goals, and engaging resources to execute the actions. A strategy describes how the result will be achieved.

Why do we need a Strategy?

If we are going to be intentional about ministry, we must engage in a matter of discipline to ensure that the end result is achieved. We are in a spiritual war, and in a war, strategy is needed so that we can fight, and win!

M.O.M., it is vital that you have a strategy for your personal prayer time. List it as first on your agenda for the day. Spend time in the presence of the Lord, where He will download instructions for how you are to navigate in life and ministry. It might help you if your personal prayer time is in the room, or on the instrument you are skilled at playing. Since God is the creator and source of all things and music reflections His greatness, what an awesome encounter you can experience!

Nothing can take the place of His presence, and M.O.M., you need His presence to facilitate your responsibility effectively. 'In earth, as it is in heaven', is the end goal, and heaven is awaiting a place within **you**, which can only be achieved through prayer and fellowship in His presence.

In 2006, I felt the leading of the Lord to initiate a fifteen minute prayer call every Sunday Morning geared specifically toward those who have been assigned to the varied facets of Levitical Arts. It became evident to me that many of them were discouraged, depleted, and needed a covering of prayer and a word of encouragement.

Musicians, dancers, choir directors, worship leaders, praise teams, media personnel, Ministers of Music, etc., gather each Sunday from all over the country at five o'clock a.m. Pacific Standard Time, to be infused with faith and inspiration as they prepare to approach their responsibility in the house of the Lord.

What started out with just a handful of individuals, now services hundreds who join the "The Levitical Prayer Call" each week, serving as impetus for the discipline to experience God before they attempt to work on His behalf. It has become a source of strength and prophetic insight, not only for those who attend but for me as well.

For the past seventeen years of conducting this call, I have been consistently reminded of the fact that the enemy has a coordinated attack aimed at the Levite. He understands the power of that position and knows that if the Levite is contaminated, it is very likely that those to whom he or she will minister to, will also get some of that residue of contamination on them.

Spending time in the presence of God in prayer will foster experiences like that of the prophet Isaiah where he experienced the glory of the Lord on a level that he had not before. As a result of seeing the holiness of God, he was then made aware of his sinfulness.

> *"Then said I, Woe is me! for I am undone; because I am a man of unclean lips, and I dwell in the midst of a people of unclean lips: for mine eyes have seen the King, the Lord of hosts. Then flew one of the seraphim unto me, having a live coal in his hand, which he had taken with the tongs from off the altar: And he laid it upon my mouth, and said, Lo, this hath touched thy lips; and thine iniquity is taken away, and thy sin purged. Also, I heard the voice of the Lord, saying, Whom shall I send, and who will go for us? Then said I, Here am I; send me."* **(Isaiah 6:5-8)**

There is no such thing as arrogance in the presence of the Lord. Once you truly **SEE** the Lord, nothing, not even what you may think of yourself can compare. It is vital that all who minister on behalf of the Lord come into fellowship with him to maintain the spirit of humility and acquire the fortitude necessary to minister as He desires.

I recall a professor at ORU who shared with his students that for every minute planned to be before the people in the preaching moment, there should be an hour of preparation attached to every minute we planned speak. He went on to say, "If you won't spend time studying, praying and then listening to God, why should the people listen to you?" These statements riveted me to my core and aided us in framing our ministry from the standpoint of preparation in the presence of God through the mode of prayer.

M.O.M., you may be facing difficulty in your ministry, feeling disappointed for one reason or another, but I admonish you, take that issue, those persons, that situation to the Lord in prayer and as He always does, He will work it out for your good and for His glory!

MASTERY OF YOUR CRAFT

1 Chronicles 15:22 .... *And Chenaniah, chief of the Levites, was for song: he instructed about the song, because he was skillful.*

M.O.M., no matter your musical instrument, vocal gift, directing agility, or organizational prowess, endeavor to master your craft ought to be of key importance to you. In 1 Chronicles chapter 15, we will note the account of the organization of David's Tabernacle.

The chapter gives us a view into the detailed and meticulous aspect of selecting those who would be appointed to minister in the Tabernacle. In verse twenty two we observe that Chenaniah was selected because he was skillful.

The definition of skill is to have the ability to do something well. Chenaniah was chosen, not only to lead the songs, but also to teach the songs to others. Chenaniah functioned as a teaching priest; one who is responsible for completing the task as assigned, but also possessing the ability to teach, posture and equip others to do likewise.

It is not enough for you M.O.M. to know what to do. Who are you training to take your place? What are you exhibiting; modeling that skill is a necessary component to success, and that it is only acquired through putting the time and work in? Who are you pouring into to ensure that the work does not stop with you?

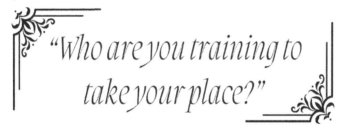

"Who are you training to take your place?"

Mastery of the craft requires – *here is that word again* – DISCIPLINE.

The first person we need to lead is ourselves and if we can do that, then we will be more likely qualified to lead someone else. We must make the time and employ the effort necessary to be the very best version of ourselves, in our roles and responsibilities.

If we are really serious about sharpening our skills, each day we should attempt to secure an element that will elevate our understanding of our craft. Formal music education and lessons in the area of desired skill will aid in your quest for excellence.

I often say that God will borrow from that which has been acquired and hidden within an individual and use it to bring Glory to His name. For instance, if a worship leader has been an ardent student of the Word of God, when it comes time for the prophetic song of the Lord, or the song of spontaneity, the Word that has been implanted in the heart will rise in that moment to be used along with the understanding of chordal and melodic structures.

Don't be afraid to reach outside of the confines of the four walls of the church to receive information that will better equip you to function more excellently in your role. Go to conferences, master classes, and seminars that are not directly related to what you do but possess the universal principles that will assist you in your quest for mastery.

Early on in my years as a M.O.M., I attended several leadership conferences, a few conducted by leadership guru, John Maxwell. Although his teachings were not specifically geared to my role as M.O.M., the leadership insights gained were immeasurable and assisted me in my quest for greater levels of excellence in my role.

Because I sought wisdom in an area not thought to be necessarily embraced in my line of work, my consciousness was expanded, my understanding of leadership concepts was sharpened, affording me a greater capacity to lead others, as well as receiving clarity to recognize those things (and people) that come to steal purpose.

Mastery is acquired by putting the work in, having "skin in the game", and putting the work in requires tremendous effort, but in the end the result will cause all the hard work and sacrifice to be worth it.

MUSICAL SELECTION & WORSHIP PLANNING

An understanding of the church's yearly liturgical calendar, including special events and the directives from P.O.P on how the church should speak to those times and seasons, is a conversation that should be had, not only between M.O.M and P.O.P, but also individuals who will have the responsibility of some level of planning participation for the success of these events.

In this season, we cannot be tentative about how we approach our worship – everything we do must be strategic and intentional.

Engaging in the conversation of exploring the importance of aligning musical selections with the themes and seasons of the church calendar, will be necessary to allow "the handle" to do its work.

P.O.P. – it is suggested that you allow the involvement of M.O.M in the planning process to allow for cohesive and purposeful worship experiences. This certainly comes into play as it relates to congregations that are multi-generational.

In addition, while planning your special services, your special days, and songs, you must remember three important things:

1) Preparing a worship 'set' should always have at the center and its core, God! It is all about Him anyway!

2) The song selections you choose for service play a vital role in gaining the attention of heaven and engaging your audience.

3) Engaging in worship is like going on a journey and it is your responsibility to take those who will experience what you have prepared with you.

In addition to serving as the President and International Minister of Music for the International Music Department (IMD) of the Church of God in Christ for twelve years, I also served for eight of those years as the Liturgist for the Church. In this role, I assisted two members of the twelve man ruling council of the church, General Board Members, Bishop G.D. McKinney and Bishop F.O. White, the leaders of the Holy Convocation Worship Planning Commission, whose responsibility it was to ensure that cohesion was maintained throughout the services, and that every aspect of the services were connected to the general theme presented for the week.

These generals in the faith mentored and shaped my understanding of the liturgical aspects of churchdom and how to effectively plan for 'high church' as well as our regular services. Verbal and written communication for months leading up to the Convocation were the norm, correspondence to those who had been selected by the Presiding Bishop was an absolute must.

This was all done to ensure that the planning of the services was met with not just the aspect of ministerial excellence, but most importantly the anointing.

As President of the IMD, I had the honor of bringing together highly skilled choir directors and creating a collective entitled the 'Quorum of Directors', whose responsibility it was to assist me in directing the C.H.

Mason Memorial Mass Choir, as well as discovering song selections that spoke to the theme which could be utilized in each part of the service. We met at least four months prior to the Holy Convocation, and from that meeting would come up with a list of at least sixty songs we could pull from, at any given time in the services.

We always had a plan.

We met with the musicians and rehearsed the choir with what our intention would be for each service. But, then there were those times when the Holy Spirit would shift the service and we had to adjust what we had planned to sing to accommodate the flow.

My team and I would huddle by my chair with the list and because we did the work beforehand, we were not ill-prepared for the shift.

"Gone are the days of just pulling something out of the arsenal because it is easy and familiar."

We could just look at the list and determine what other song would be appropriate for the moment.

We planned and because we did, we were prepared.

Gone are the days of just pulling something out of the arsenal because it is easy and familiar – our worship planning and subsequent song selection deserve some time and effort for the maximum result of exceptionality to be achieved.

As I bring this section to a close, allow me to present an example of how we ought to approach the thought for preparation in our song selections. Within the next few pages, you will find a correspondence crafted to address the directors in my local church regarding the same.

This example is not presented to state that this is the only way to do so, but hopefully some of these pointers can assist you in your pursuit of excellence.

Good Day Team -

With great challenges come great opportunities to allow our creativity to cause what may seem like a deficit to others, be revealed ultimately to us as a blessing. At this juncture, there are some foundational elements which must be reiterated and underscored, so we can move in a greater dimension toward optimal excellence.

Effectively immediately, all proposed material for all singing aggregations must be submitted 1 (one) month prior to ministry. The office and I are working on a 2 (two) month schedule, which will be given 1 (one) month in advance of the present month, so that each of you will have knowledge of when you are scheduled to minister.

Whether you have the opportunity to minister or not in the coming month, it would be good to have an arsenal of well thought out, planned music, which will assist me in the goal of creating a musical "production" for each service we embark upon.

This practice will also possess the following benefits –

1) We will all be on one accord, flexible and better prepared for any possible changes.

2) This will also allow us to disseminate approved material to our choir members, praise team, musicians, and office staff in a timely manner.

In our efforts to synchronize the *"sound of the house"* each director and praise & worship leader is to make it a point to implement the following principles when selecting material for ministry.

PRAISE & WORSHIP LEADERS

1) Select material that the congregation can effortlessly sing along to; not having to rely necessarily on lyrics on the screen.

2) Songs MUST NOT depend on musical syncopation to cause the song to "win". Praise & Worship must always be **simple** enough for the congregation not to feel

intimidated to attempt to sing. *REMEMBER – Praise & Worship is the song of the people to the Lord.* Often, the rhythms and syncopation take the attention away from the meaning of the song.

3) In maintaining the Spirit and tone of the house – choose material that convey and are in alignment with the vision of the house. In addition, remember the sound of the "Saints in Praise" series. (*We will discuss this at length when we meet*)

CHOIR DIRECTORS

1) Select material relative to the specific musical aggregation you have been assigned to, ensuring that the material is in the proper key and tempo for the demographic.

2) The full scope of the proposed ministry performance for that aggregation, must be fully disclosed and conveyed to my office. (i.e. - All leads, special recitations etc.)

3) Due to the fact that there is currently 1 (one) rehearsal in most cases, please ensure that the time you do have with the volunteers is utilized efficiently, by being prepared to teach effectively.

We have drafted a new fillable song submittal form which includes a field to add the link of the music being proposed. If there is an original song, please ensure that it is converted to and MP3, and/or provide the office with a CD.

I appreciate each one of your efforts. We are workers together and with your assistance, we can "Make His Praise Glorious!"

A FRESH SOUND

In environments where there is a mutual respect and cohesive relationship between M.O.M and P.O.P, I've found that the music is fresh – like a pure spring of water. I am pretty sure that there are more reasons for the purity of sound, but more often than not, the factor of a healthy relationship between number 1 and number 2 is a prime reason for the music of the church ministering to the soul and the spirit. It ministers on a level beyond the ear, beyond the ability to recognize excellence in its presentation.

On the other hand, I have visited churches that are led by controlling Pastors; and I have always found the music to be less impactful than desired.

Honor is a huge deal! When the P.O.P honors the M.O.M, there is a release of the gifts that are within M.O.M to assist the P.O.P. in achieving the goal, great accomplishments are achieved.

Many Pastors do not recognize the power they have when they release the trusted, tried, and true M.O.M. to go forth in ministry. It makes your job easier P.O.P.

To reiterate, if your M.O.M. is trusted, loyal and has proven themselves to be in line with the agenda of God that has been given to you, allow them to be free to facilitate the worship and watch how God will lift you and give you ease.

M.O.M, once that responsibility and trust is bestowed, it is your responsibility not to take advantage of it. Be honorable in your dealings and make sure that nothing you are doing will cause your P.O.P. to distrust you or your motives.

When it comes to the ministry moment, minister within the requested time restraints and cause those whom you are responsible for and serve alongside you do the same.

Don't get so wrapped up in the spirit that you lose sense of time. God is a God of order and if you have been given an allotted amount of time to minister and you sense that there is more the Lord wants to do in that moment, attempt to get the P.O.P's permission to extend the time prior to moving forward. *"The spirits of the prophets are subject to the prophets"* (1Corinthians 14:32) and *"Let all things be done decently and in order"* (I Corinthians 14:40)

These types of scenarios and possibilities should be discussed with the P.O.P. prior to the ministry moment and you both should come to an agreement on some sort of signal which will indicate that something unplanned is getting ready to happen.

M.O.M., in the context of a worship service, it is your responsibility to be so connected and in sync with P.O.P, that even if you can't see their responses, you can feel them in the spirit. I have personally experienced this with Pastors I have worked with over the years, whether the role is that of M.O.M., or visiting psalmist.

As a visiting psalmist, I must recognize that there is a sound of the house and, it is vital that I deliver what I have been invited for but do it within the established spiritual protocol which has been established in that house.

A fresh sound does not necessarily constitute singing the top 40, Christian songs on the Billboard charts. Just because other churches are singing it, does not mean that it aligns with the mission and the sound of the house in which you serve. M.O.M, you will need to spend time in prayer in addition to reviewing the lyrics and examining the general message of the song to ascertain if it fits within the parameters of the sound of the house.

> *"The sound of the house is not just musical, but spiritual as well."*

Early on in my days of assuming the role of Minister of Music at West Angeles, Bishop Blake and I would meet periodically to review songs he was exposed to elsewhere that he felt would be appropriate for the music ministry to add to our repertoire.

I then began to search for material similar to what he shared with me and thus, continued crafting the ever-evolving sound of the house.

The sound of the house is not just musical, but spiritual as well, which underscores the importance of recalling and rehearsing what heaven has been releasing to a house over a period of time.

In a musical sense, it is necessary to offer to the congregation worship songs with simple melodies as often as possible. The songs the congregation will sing to the Lord should be expressions of their gratitude and sentiments to the Father, without convoluted melodies, complex harmonies, or difficult syncopations. With choir music, you may select pieces more intricate in nature, as the choir is usually well-rehearsed, trained and expected to be able to execute more difficult material with a greater measure of precision.

As previously expressed, the sound of the house is not just musical, but also spiritual. Understanding the spiritual aspects of songs and the importance of *"Speaking to yourselves in psalms and hymns and spiritual songs, singing and making melody in your heart to the Lord;"* (Ephesians 5:19), can lift the worship gathering from a perfunctory experience to an encounter where heaven touches earth.

SELAH

Feel free to write on this page how Chapter Five spoke to you.

_____

_____

_____

_____

_____

_____

_____

_____

_____

_____

_____

_____

_____

CHAPTER SIX

PARTING THOUGHTS

GIVE THANKS

A grateful heart is a thankful heart!
> *In everything give thanks: for this is the will of God in Christ Jesus concerning you.* **(1 Thessalonians 5:18)**

Let's pause here and pray together –

෩෩

Heavenly Father, we come to you with hearts full of gratitude, admiration, and appreciation.

We are so thankful for the way You have revealed Your plan and Your Kingdom in our lives and praise You for removing anything that could hinder that plan, our progress, and our growth.

Even though we may be in familiar surroundings, we recognize Father, that this is a season of change.

We eagerly welcome the new opportunities for growth, and positive transformation you have in store for us.
We wholeheartedly embrace the guidance of your Holy Spirit and are incredibly grateful for the fresh work you are doing in our lives.

Thank You, Father, for helping us understand our purpose and for giving us the freedom to fulfill that purpose with excellence.

Help us to remain focused on the assignment and not to be distracted by the tactics of the enemy. We are grateful and humbled by Your faithfulness to Your word over our lives.

We thank You that it shall come to pass!
We are so thankful from the bottom of our hearts.

AMEN!!!

ⱥⱥⱥ

You may ask, "Why is there a prayer of thanks that begins this section?" It was done intentionally to remind us all that there is never an inappropriate time to give God thanks.

In addition, the prayer was inserted in this **sixth** chapter, because I am reminded of what David modeled as the Ark of the Covenant was being brought back into the city of Jerusalem in 2 Samuel chapter six verse thirteen.

> *"And it was so, that when they that bare the ark of the Lord had gone six paces, he sacrificed oxen and fatlings. "* (2 Samuel 6:13)

Six steps then an offering, Six steps then the giving of thanks. Can you imagine how long that journey was?

Every six steps, there was an offering of thanksgiving, and not just lifting hands and speaking well of the Lord, there was the actual slaying of animals. The Hebrew word for thanks is "Todah", which also reflects a sacrifice as the words of thanks are being rendered.

Likewise, M.O.M., we should find ourselves in a consistent state of thanksgiving and gratitude to the

"We should find ourselves in a consistent state of thanksgiving and gratitude to the Lord."

Lord for who He is, and what He is doing in our lives. Why? Because it puts us in the posture of receptivity, which is needed for what we have been assigned to do. We must always be open to the Spirit of God to cause His purpose to be revealed through us.

M.O.M., you have made it thus far, God did not bring you to this place and time in your life and ministry to leave you. No matter what you have experienced in the past, it was given to help shape you and you must choose to give thanks as opposed to complain.

Do you remember how the children of Israel remained in the wilderness for forty years because of their murmuring and complaining? I am certain that you do not wish to experience delays because of complaining about your situation.

This is not the time to waste time – we must be about our Father's business and now that we know better, don't go back to what we used to know and do.

Don't Go Back

Imagine with me a well, which provides fresh water to a community; a dependable well - a well that everybody goes to, to receive and be refreshed.

Now imagine that well being stopped up. What are the town's people and establishments to do? Can they receive water from another source? Sure, but **that well** in **that community** was designed to be there to provide the necessary resource of water to them, right where they were.

Quite a while ago, I had a vision of a stopped-up well, being dug out. I could not ascertain the depth of the well from the surface, but because of the length of time it took, it was obvious that it was a very deep well.

As the well was being excavated by the hand of God, He dug until He hit water and as the water began to flow, it filled the well. The depth of the well was synonymous with the potential that it had for water capacity.

I believe this vision is synonymous with God removing that which would stop His flow in our lives. It represents us allowing Him, to process us for His Glory.

When the LORD begins to remove things from our lives, it is important that we don't go back looking for it; just let it be because the removal of those things has now created greater capacity for the Glory to flow through you. The Father is **changing** YOU!

Growing up as an adolescent in Cambria Heights, NY, one of my chores was to assist my father in our backyard. My father kept a very healthy garden, and we would often see lots of caterpillars.

Some of the caterpillars were good for the vegetation, and then there were others that were not that good for his garden, that we had to get rid of.

One of my Father's prized possessions in his garden was the huge pear tree which sat in the corner – North/West of the garden.

I believe that area was significant because it seemed as if this particular species of caterpillar just loved that pear tree and subsequently the areas surrounding that North-West corner of the garden.

We would go into the backyard at certain times of the year and observe the various stages of the process from the Egg to the Caterpillar, to the Pupa, or the Chrysalis ultimately, to the Butterfly. My father showed me how to safely pick up the chrysalis, so as not to wound or cause it any harm. So, we would carefully pick the chrysalis up from the bottom, and when we picked it up, it would squirm on the inside; I learned that it wasn't in pain; it was just yielding to the process that was taking place on the inside.

After our careful examination of the chrysalis, we would put it back on the leaf of the pear tree, or back in the dirt where it originally was. Days later we would return to see the chrysalis shell on the ground, but we could not find the Butterfly.

The process of Caterpillar to Butterfly consisted of the Caterpillar resorbing within itself in the chrysalis, to begin the transformation into something more beautiful than it was before. The Butterfly has the same DNA as it did when it was a Caterpillar, but can never go back to being a Caterpillar, because now, it is a new creation!

The Apostle Paul reminds us in 2 Corinthians 5:17 –

> *"Therefore, if any man be in Christ, he is a new creature: old things are passed away; behold, all things are become new"*

DO NOT GO BACK to what you used to be! Do not go back to what you used to think. Do not go back to **how you used to respond**; once God delivers you, Do not go back to the things that brought you solace, although they may have seemed to be good. The chrysalis was good for the butterfly at one point in its' life, because it served the purpose of assisting in the process of formation, however for the Butterfly to reach its fulfillment, it had to let go of the past and move forward!

M.O.M - God is calling you to another place of anointing, a place of the elevation of your mind, of who you are, what you can do, and what He has called you to be. The Father is bringing us to a place of acceleration, and for some of us we can't even fathom that, because we are looking back.

We are looking back at what we used to be, and what we used to do, and because we're in the same circumstances we can't see beyond where we sit right now, but listen, we may be in the same spot, but we are in a different season. **DO NOT LOOK BACK**.

Philippians 3:13&14

*13 Brethren, I count not myself to have apprehended: but this one thing I do, **forgetting those things which are behind**, and **reaching forth** unto those things which are before, 14 I press toward the mark for the prize of the high calling of God in Christ Jesus.*

Paul said in essence - I have not reached my zenith, I'm not all the way there, but **this one thing I do, I forget those things which are behind**.

M.O.M – you may have been having a difficult time forgetting those things that have transpired. The enemy consistently brings up what happened in the past, but let's take a lesson from the Caterpillar - forget those things which are behind and reach forward to those things which are before. There is something bigger and better right around the corner.

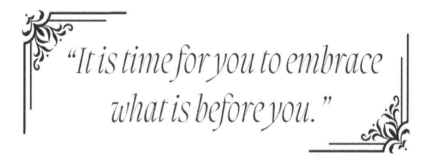

"It is time for you to embrace what is before you."

The Heavenly Father is showing you something that He's had in His heart for you, and you cannot receive it because you're looking at where you are. You are stifled due to your preconceived limitations, but it's time for you to embrace what is before you.

In this season, people are hungry for an authentic encounter with God. They are looking for something beyond 'church as usual', all of the pomp and circumstance of what **WE** have made, a relationship with God to look like.

It is time for Pastors and Ministers of Music to realize that their relationship and the synergy between the two is a vital and necessary component of the conduit for the flow of God during our worship services.

I trust that through reading this book, you are now postured to do better, be better and expect better.

May the principles in this book guide you to the path of increased success in your ministry as you M.O.M., and you P.O.P embrace each other in the role which God has ordained you both to walk in, for the advancement of the Kingdom right where you are!

SELAH

AFTERWORD

Reflecting upon the diverse influences in my life, both spiritual and musical, I am grateful that I was not confined to one style/idiom of music, or Christian spiritual expression. Through these varied experiences, I have gained a broad spectrum of knowledge, allowing me to better understand how the Kingdom of God is expressed through music.

To my fellow Ministers of Music, I leave you with a heartfelt prayer. May you remain *"steadfast, unmovable, and always abound in the work of the Lord. Remember, your labor is not in vain in the Lord's eyes"* (1 Corinthians 15:58).

As you continue to support the vision of your Pastor, I encourage you to embrace **your** Godly aspirations and tap into the greatness within you. You are more than what you have become, and the time to rise to your fullest potential is now!

Heaven eagerly awaits your emergence, for it is through you that the sound of God can resound throughout the earth. Your Pastor eagerly anticipates your growth, as the Word of God can be sown into well-prepared soil each week. The congregation eagerly awaits your ministry, as they thirst for the mighty river of God to flow through you.

And as for me, I stand in anticipation of witnessing and hearing testimonies of the incredible manifestation of God's greatness revealed in you!

Embrace this journey of music ministry, and let your unique voice resound, for the world is waiting to be touched by the power of God through you.

Finally – I leave you Numbers 6:24-26, the Aaronic blessing which Aaron the high priest spoke over the children of Israel.

May this blessing follow you wherever you go –

THE LORD BLESS THEE, AND KEEP THEE:
THE LORD MAKE HIS FACE SHINE UPON THEE,
AND BE GRACIOUS UNTO THEE:
THE LORD LIFT UP HIS COUNTENANCE
UPON THEE,
AND GIVE THEE PEACE.

Both now and forever more,

Amen.

ॐ

Made in the USA
Columbia, SC
27 January 2024

30974304R00085